Sparks in Love

From the author of the TheSoda-Pop.com™

Sparks in Love

A SURVIVOR'S STORY

SUSAN SPARKS

Published in the United States by Bright Light Books

Bright Light Books
4075 Park Boulevard
BRIGHT
·LIGHT·   Suite 102-113
BOOKS   San Diego, CA 92103

Disclaimer
As in any first-person account, the events in this book are from a single perspective, the author's. The minds and memories of others were not accessible. With respect for the privacy of others, she has changed names, a few locations, occupations, and descriptions, but the impact and essence of events is true as she remembers them.

ISBN: 978-1-7324408-0-7
Mobi ISBN: 978-1-7324408-2-1
Ebook ISBN: 978-1-7324408-1-4

Publisher's Cataloging-In-Publication Data
(Prepared by The Donohue Group, Inc.)

Names: Sparks, Susan (Writer on domestic abuse)
Title: Sparks in love / Susan Sparks.
Description: First edition. | San Diego, CA : Bright Light Books, [2018]
Identifiers: ISBN 9781732440807 | ISBN 9781732440814 (ebook) | ISBN 9781732440821
     (mobi)
Subjects: LCSH: Sparks, Susan--Marriage. | Abused wives. | Family violence. | Man-woman
     relationships.
Classification: LCC HV6626 .S63 2018 (print) | LCC HV6626 (ebook) | DDC 362.82/92--dc23

Printed in the United States of America

Library of Congress Control Number: 2018953360

FIRST EDITION

Cover and interior design by GKS Creative, Nashville, TN.

I dedicate this book to my two incredible boys - whom I hope will never see or read it - and will at no time have to fully understand why mom tried to change the world.
Your strength of character is my inspiration.

And...

To my sisterhood, my fellow "one in fours," you are the reason that this book exists. I share with you this quote in the hopes that you will gain the same strength from it that I have:

"You can't go back and make a new start,
but you can start right now and make a brand new ending."
JAMES R. SHERMAN

You are not alone.

S. Sparks

Her Future Was Bright

There was a place within me, and it was so strong,
And I'm trying to find it, but it's missing so long.
There was a place within me, that drove me there,
And no one could stop me 'cause I didn't care.
There was a place within her, for she was so strong,
But I cannot find it, she's been missing so long.
And all of my days and all of my nights
Are spent going back to see the old sights.
I look so hard to see through her eyes, before she got weak with
*   sadness and cries.*
How did she do it and where was her drive,
It was automatic, she was so alive.
She made her mind up and then she was there,
She didn't need help, she didn't need prayer.
But now I call out and I try hard to find,
The person I left years ago in my mind.
I want to know her, I want to see, how she was so strong before I
*   became me.*
For she took me there, and never was weak,
Her future was bright before mine was bleak.
There was a place within me, that I need to go find,
Before I can put my future behind.

S. Sparks

THE FIFTEEN WARNING SIGNS OF DOMESTIC ABUSE

1. *Tells you that you can never do anything right*

2. *Shows extreme jealousy of your friends and time spent away*

3. *Keeps you or discourages you from seeing friends or family members*

4. *Insults, demeans, or shames you with put-downs*

5. *Controls every penny spent in the household*

6. *Takes your money or refuses to give you money for necessary expenses*

7. *Looks at you or acts in ways that scare you*

8. *Controls who you see, where you go, or what you do*

9. *Prevents you from making your own decisions*

10. *Tells you that you are a bad parent or threatens to harm or take away your children*

11. *Prevents you from working or attending school*

12. *Destroys your property or threatens to hurt or kill your pets*

13. *Intimidates you with guns, knives, or other weapons*

14. *Pressures you to have sex when you don't want to, or do things sexually you're not comfortable with*

15. *Pressures you to use drugs or alcohol*

Source: The National Domestic Violence HOTLINE/thehotline.org

HuffPost.com

38,028,000

The number of women in the U.S. who have experienced physical intimate partner violence in their lifetimes.

Nearly half of all women in U.S. (48.4%)
have experienced at least one form of psychological aggression by an intimate partner during their lifetime, with 40.3% reporting some form of expressive aggression (e.g., their partner acted angry in a way that seemed dangerous, told them they were a loser or a failure, insulted or humiliated them), or some form of coercive control (41.1%) by an intimate partner.

Source: National Intimate Partner and Sexual Violence Survey, 2010 Summary Report. National Center for Injury Prevention and Control, Division of Violence Prevention, Atlanta, GA, and Control of the Centers for Disease Control and Prevention.

---

up to 75% of abused women who are murdered are killed after they leave their partners

Source: www.theguardian.com

National Coalition for the Homeless

70x

The number of times more likely a woman in the U.S is to be murdered in the few weeks after leaving her abusive partner than at any other time in the relationship.

I was one of those women. I was potentially all of those women. And now, having escaped from my marriage of two decades and suffered through an often painful and continuously abusive divorce proceeding, I am healing.

Who are you that you picked up this book and what is your why? Are you a young woman dating a man who mesmerizes you even as he shames you with putdowns? Are you a woman in a relationship you feel you need even while you know, from somewhere deep inside, that it is truly toxic? Are you beginning to question how you got to where you are? Or are you a married woman – perhaps with children – who woke up one day and no longer recognized herself in the mirror? Are you trying so hard to please, so hard to make him love you that you are no longer sure exactly who you are anymore?

And what is he doing to you? Is your self-respect being eroded by a man who should be grateful to have you in his life? Are you hiding this from the outside world while you slowly crumble from within? Are you a powerful executive – respected and listened to at work but constantly chastised at home? Are you a mom, embarrassed and demeaned in front of your children every day? Are you a student? A volunteer? Someone trying to improve herself, or the world around her, while he tries to break you, telling you that you are worthless?

Have you been separated from your family, your friends, and allowed it to happen just to keep the peace?

Are you more focused on protecting your children from seeing what is happening than you are on protecting yourself?

Do you cry in private while putting on a brave face with those outside your home? Does your oh-so-perfect family hide a dirty secret – the secret of abuse?

If you said yes to any or all of the above, then you are me and I am you. And I know exactly how you feel and I already know why you picked up this book. We are members of a sisterhood that we never asked to join. We are members of a group who desperately need to be properly educated, helped, and then abolished forever – the sisterhood of abused women.

It is with this in mind that I share my story. To let you know you are not alone, to let you know you are worthy, to let you know there is a way out and a bright future beyond...and to help you successfully navigate the road to safety and freedom.

I am Susan Sparks, and what follows is my story.

PROLOGUE

Part I

Hitting the Bottom... Stair

When I see her laying on the bottom stair, her body is twisted in a shape that does not look human. I imagine them making a chalk outline around her and everyone gathering to try and figure out her story. Only she is not dead yet. She lies there for forty minutes in terror and finally hears that she will get an ambulance. Then, her mother is on the way. He gives in and doesn't try to move her when she howls, but he comes near her several times and the terror is almost more than she can take. She is totally helpless. She almost passes out, but wills herself to stay present. All the while her children stand watching from the landing above, asking her over and over if she is ok. The words she screams in her head never reach their tiny ears. They take her out on a stretcher and she feels the air come back into her lungs. She knows she is alive. She knows that this all means something, but she is not sure yet what it is. For years they will ask her if he pushed her down the stairs. Friends, neighbors, people she barely even knows will stop her in odd places at odd times to try and get to the truth. Later she will realize that he did not, he wasn't even there, but something did. She wants to make sense of it, but now she can only lay back and listen as the EMT looks down at her and gently speaks: "Do not move, keep breathing, what is your name, do you know where you are?"

She thinks about it carefully for the next four years and tries to make sense of it all, but something will not let it come together in her mind. There is too much pain, too much tragedy, things she cannot say out loud yet and cannot admit even to herself, silently, inside of her own mind. She somehow knows that to put it together could be her undoing, so she chooses to stuff it down, keep it locked away, and not deal with it.

Until one day she realizes that the cost she is paying to suppress it is now more than she can afford. She can't stay quiet any longer because she feels it bubbling up. She knows within her heart that she is here to say something and to make a difference in this world because why else would this have possibly happened to her? At that moment in time she jumps out of bed and runs to her computer and it all comes spilling out in precise detail, in powerful sentences. She can't stop the words from coming and she can't stop the tears from coming; they are in perfect harmony, like a symphony suppressed by a maestro for far too many years. She is a writer and this is her way to heal. She writes a blog, her very first, and then realizes that she has just changed her own life. It's time to come out and tell the world what has happened to her. There is no more hiding from the truth. Today is the day.

This is her story and so it is mine. These words document the torture, torment, and triumph of living through and escaping domestic abuse. They are living breathing true accounts of a life that goes on because she would not quit, will not quit, and does not quit. I am Susan Sparks and I am ready to tell my story now. I am a real person with a real story and it is one that will not end until I see that the one in four women who will experience domestic abuse in her lifetime start to understand that they have a choice: to escape, to avoid, or to heal. And so, I am here to do my part with you: to help, to hope, and to heal.

I live my days feeling like many people rolled into one. I am a survivor, a mother, a daughter, a sister, and a friend to many. Some even call me a role model, although I'm not sure of that. The magnitude of that thought is both humbling and overwhelming. I am a person here to tell my story so it does not become yours. If it is yours, then I want to help you change it. If it was yours, then I want to show you that you, too, can write a new ending.

For years I hid my life, my pain, my torment behind the closed doors of my large suburban home because I was ashamed of what was happening to me. I hid it for so long that I could no longer separate what it was and what I was, and so it became a part of me. I have traveled a long and painful journey, and from the other side I work to slowly unravel what happened and try to break it apart from who I am now. It feels to me like a surgeon trying to separate conjoined twins. Where is the heart connected? The brain? Can we separate them and still have one life left? Will she have a complete heart? A mind that can lead her through the rest of her days?

Yes, it can be done. But the work involved will take years. It has taken years. It's been four since I fled from that home, and it is only now that I am strong enough to put my fingers on the keyboard and begin to tell you what happened to me. I've wrestled with whether or not to do this. But I know that I must because I am living in a way that others tell me every day is noteworthy. They tell me that they are inspired by me. They tell me that they are proud. They tell me how sorry they are, and they tell me how wonderful it is that I have taken a life so cracked and broken and rebuilt it into what I now have.

If I have done this, then you can, too. Because I am in no way any more special, any stronger, or different than you. Maybe I just got here first.

So, thank you for taking this journey with me. I don't want to do it alone. It is dark and scary and horrifying to go back. But I go back for you, I go back for me, and I go back for the one in four women who will suffer from domestic abuse in her lifetime. We are not alone. Let us all pray, let us all heal, and let us all become one together.

This day I run to my computer to write, to unload. *Did he push you down the stairs?* It was one of the most important stories I could share because it was the day I literally hit bottom. I hit the bottom of my life, I hit the bottom of my abuse, and I hit the bottom of my foyer staircase after going airborne from the top landing. And every single day and event after that changed my life, forever. I share it with you because by understanding this you will understand the beginning of my end. Here is where we start our journey together.

Did he push you down the stairs?

In November of 2011 I had a tragic accident. Our beautiful dog was sleeping in the foyer, no longer able to walk up the stairs to come to sleep in our bedroom. I had already put my younger son to bed for the night, and it was time to take my older son up. We were going up the stairs and singing happy songs, and as we reached the top I turned around and saw the sadness in my dog's eyes because he wanted to come up to bed, too. My then-husband was in our basement theatre room watching a movie and having a grand old time while I, (as usual), was running the house. I turned quickly, too quickly, to race down the stairs and carry our dog up so we could all go up together, and I lost my balance.

Time stood still as I felt first my left foot and then my right foot go swinging out in front of me. I desperately grabbed for the handrail and missed. From there I fell from the top landing all the way down to the bottom landing, square on my right upper arm, smashing it to pieces. The pain was indescribable.

My bone was in three separate pieces. I couldn't move. I couldn't talk. I could only moan when talked to, and I was moaning loudly. My son ran to the basement to get my husband who yelled at him for interrupting the movie and barked, "This better not be a joke!" as he came storming up the stairs. He found me crumpled and broken and looking up at him with desperate pleading eyes. He asked me if I could move. He came toward me and I howled in fear. Clearly inconvenienced, he wanted me to be ok, but I wasn't. He finally called an ambulance and off I went. My mom came rushing over to watch the boys, and my husband drove over to the ER to meet us there.

The injury was so bad that they wanted to do surgery in the morning. They also gave me the choice to heal on my own, without pins and screws in my bone for the rest of my life, so I took the hard road but the one that I knew would make me feel the best in the long run. It took two hours and an IV full of morphine before they could even attempt to move me for an X-ray. And there, in the middle of it all, my husband turned to me and said, with a face full of disgust, "I can already see it now. You're going to milk this for all it's worth." And in response to this, right there on my ER bed, I quietly began to cry.

What had happened? I can explain this to you in simple terms. His world imploded. His world? Yep. His world. His world where I did all of the housework, took care of our children, cooked, cleaned, ran our home, and corresponded with school and doctors and the outside world, all flashed before his eyes. He was going to have to do something to help. And there was more, it got worse for him. Our isolated existence, behind closed doors, that no one was privy to, was going to have to open up. People were going to have to come in and help me. I only had one working arm and needed a lot of pain pills, and I was put on bed rest for months. This was a disaster for him!

My husband did what only someone totally self-centered can do in such a situation. He moved out of our bedroom and he never spoke a single word to me during my recovery. He found a way to further isolate, degrade, humiliate, and make me feel like a stranger in my own home. Since I was unable to perform what he saw as my role in his world, he shut me out. And he did so at a time when I needed him more than I ever had in our twenty years together.

The details from here are very hard to discuss; they are painful, they are ugly, and they still sting. It is incredibly difficult to be so weak and so helpless and in so much pain; having the man who is supposed to love you turn on you only exacerbates that pain.

My mom moved in to help, and my husband decided he would only speak to her. He spoke not one single word to me in twelve weeks. NOT ONE. My mom slept on the sofa in my bedroom and took care of me at night. I would sleep during the day and wake up the minute the boys came home from school. I would help them with their homework, eat dinner with them, and tend to them as much as possible. All while their father made a point of ignoring me in front of them.

We know when things are wrong in our lives, and we know when we need to make a change, to step away. But too often, particularly if we are in an abusive situation, we find ourselves motionless. We stand still and look for ways to make things better. We search our souls to see what we did to cause what is happening. We vest and invest in believing something good can and will come of a deteriorating situation, long past the time we should. The energy we need to extricate ourselves remains present, suppressed only by our disassociation from the reality of our circumstances. But when catastrophe finally hits, when something happens we cannot explain away, that energy becomes kinetic. It is then that we finally find the motivation, strength, and courage to say enough, and let that energy move us forward.

The fall I took was in itself a catastrophe. But it was in my husband's cold and blatant disregard for me that I found motivation. It was during this time that I finally went from indecision to decision. As soon as I was strong enough and back on my feet, I was leaving this man forever. Once I made this decision, I never looked back. It was the easiest one of my life. Why it took so long, well, that's the cycle of abuse.

When someone abuses us, particularly when the abuse is emotional, we tend to withhold knowledge of it from family and friends. Part of it is a disconnect; it is difficult to believe that someone who should love us can treat us so badly. And part of it is embarrassment; we wonder if we are worthy of better treatment or if there is something wrong with us, something that demands we be treated as inferior.

For months after my accident the community watched me make my recovery. They brought meals and flowers, and many came over to keep me company while our kids were at school. No one knew that my husband had stopped speaking to me or how debilitating his heartless behavior was for me. I was weak and embarrassed; but no one seemed to notice anything amiss, and I certainly wasn't about to share, so life went on as usual as I could keep it.

By the summer of 2012 I had made a total recovery, and in August of 2012 my birthday present to myself was my grand announcement that I wanted a divorce. He tried to talk me out of it and said he would change. I had heard that so many times before that I no longer bought into it; I would not change my mind this time. But I didn't have a plan, and this became a grave mistake. One that I will have to live with for the rest of my life. One that I will wait to tell another day.

When school started in the fall for my children, word spread of our divorce. I had many friends in this community. At certain times and during certain quiet moments, people would come up to me and ask, "Did he...did he push you down the stairs?" I have to tell you that I was grateful that they asked rather than assumed; neither I nor my children needed rumors. I love my community and I got so much strength from them. I answered each and every one of them and made sure the truth was out there.

When people sometimes still ask me, "Did he..." I answer them with a smile and say, "No, but I think God may have." I had put up with so much for so long, what else could God do but push me down those stairs in order to get that reaction from my husband and show me so clearly what my life had turned into? What I had turned into?

Something needed to happen to make me take action because I just wasn't getting there on my own.

It is not easy to recall these memories; the pain of doing so is visceral. I do it to share my story and to say this: God may not be available to push you down the stairs, so I would like to help. Well, not literally, but you know what I mean. Here I am, let me give you a push: how bad has your life gotten?

Remember this: STRENGTH + SUPPORT + PLAN = FREEDOM. You can do this.

I close my laptop and think about how much work is ahead of me. I want to provide education about domestic abuse and how to get out safely if you are stuck. I think of the stories I will need to share in an attempt to show others how not to fall into the same trap that I did, and give survivors hope. And I understand and accept the pain I will endure as I walk backwards through my life, and do the only thing I can do at this point, which is to try to understand that it truly was not my fault, and help others to do the same.

There is also the overwhelming fact that I will need to hide my identity in order to keep myself and my family safe and protect the new life that I am desperately trying to build each and every day. Safety first, I need to get it right this time.

And then, in a true and pure and brave moment in my life, I open my laptop back up, glance over the blog one final time, put my fingers on the "SEND" button, and gently press it.

I did it. There is nowhere to go now but forward. Here I am world, Susan Sparks, nice to meet you. Let's go tell a story and start to change the world of domestic abuse that lives closer to most of us than we even realize.

Part II

My Secret Had a Name

I see her at her annual OB/GYN appointment. She is dressed perfectly, as always. Her hair is perfect, her makeup is perfect. She has the perfect exterior to hide the interior that she will not let anyone see. She arrives early for her appointment, always early, never late, never letting herself upset anyone by inconveniencing them.

She walks in with a bright smile, signs in at the front desk, and takes a chair. People notice her. She is pretty, she is kind to the staff, and she makes a joke or two to let the world know that she is doing fine. She waits to be called back for her exam.

She has no idea that her life is about to change forever. That she is about to see something that will immediately alter who she is, how she thinks, and what she tells herself at night when she just can't take another day. I watch her sit there, so together, so in charge, and I wonder how she ever did it. I marvel at her strength of mind, of will, and of character. Family first, appearances matter; she did not. My heart breaks for her as I know what is about to happen, but she does not yet. A simple stop in the bathroom that will forever change every single day for the rest of her life.

They call her name and I watch her get up. I want to yell "NO!" but I know that I can't – and would I anyway if I could? This is her path, this is her destiny, and somehow, she has to walk it. I see her get up and go towards the doorway as they call her for her appointment. I watch her walk through that door knowing that she will never be the same.

A simple stop in the bathroom and a moment is frozen forever in time. Her life is about to unravel and now I can only watch her and feel so badly for her. "I'm sorry!" I want to shout it out, "I am so sorry, Susan!" But I only watch as the memory of that day plays over and over in my mind.

She is me and I am she, and this is a day that I will remember forever.

There are 15 distinct signs of domestic abuse. I didn't know that when I woke up that day. I didn't know it when I entered the doctor's office. But simply reading those signs would change my destiny.

It is the day I found out who I was. But it would take four long years and a near-tragic accident to make me come to terms with it, and to decide that I needed to take it and make it something that would help change the world into a better place.

There are 15 distinct signs of domestic abuse, and before my work is done, the world will know each and every one of them.

_____

The Day My Water Broke

It was a day that forever changed my life. I had my annual OB/GYN appointment and after being called back for my appointment they asked me if I had to use the bathroom. I did. I went into the bathroom and started juggling my purse, my keys, and my bottle of water, looking for a place to set everything down.

As I turned around, I saw this huge poster on the door. I didn't really realize what I was looking at, just this long list. Things started popping out at me like, "extreme jealousy," and "keeps you or discourages you from seeing your friends or family members" and "controls every penny spent in the household," and I thought, "That sounds like my life, what is this?"

Then I kept reading the list and it said more things like, "tells you that you can never do anything right," and "insults, demeans or shames you with put downs," and "tells you that you are a bad parent." Feeling a little uncomfortable, I thought, "This is my life. What is this?" I scanned up to the top of the poster and it said, "If you have three or more of the following signs, you are a victim of domestic abuse. Please get help today."

I dropped my purse. I dropped my keys. I dropped my water bottle on the floor. The bottle cracked, spilling water everywhere. My life - my terrible, awful daily existence of a life - had a name? It was something? I was a victim of domestic abuse? Wasn't that when you went home and hid behind the sofa so you wouldn't get hit that night? This was something different. Domestic Abuse. I was a victim of DOMESTIC ABUSE. I WAS A VICTIM OF DOMESTIC ABUSE.

My hands were shaking as I started cleaning up the water and shoving items into my purse. As I stood up from the floor I saw a stack of pamphlets in the same bright purple color as the poster that said, "For more information on Domestic Abuse..." and I quickly grabbed one and stuffed it into the bottom of my purse. The nurse knocked on the door to ask me if I was ok, and I said, "yes."

I silently went through my exam that day and every time the doctor asked me how I was doing I did what I always did: "I'm fine," I said with a smile. "Everything is fine." Except everything was not. I had a secret that I had been hiding for over a decade, and now my secret had a name, and somehow it having a name made it real. I didn't just have a terrible life, I had thirteen of the fifteen warning signs of domestic abuse listed on that poster that said you needed three to qualify. I had thirteen. *I am something, I thought to myself. I am a victim. I am a victim of domestic abuse.*

I stumbled through days, months, before I could make myself pull that pamphlet out of my purse. But one day, after hours of him yelling, berating, and intimidating me again, I went into my closet and took that pamphlet out. I read every word. Yes, this is me, I thought. This is still me. Now what do I do?

Remember this: STRENGTH + SUPPORT + PLAN = FREEDOM. You can do this.

I take a deep breath and will myself to have the courage to publish this blog, to share my private fears with others who may be struggling without somehow sapping the strength that I have worked so hard to gain. To put these words together is one thing. To send them to the Internet for the world to read is another. What if he was right? What if I was worthless and had nothing of value to say? Who would want to read this anyway? It wasn't any easier the second time than the first.

For years, people will question me about why I stayed, how I survived, and what I am doing to heal. The answer is right in front of all of us: I am writing a book and blogging about domestic abuse so that my story does not become yours. And if it already is yours, then let's rewrite the ending together. It is never too late. You just need to learn what you are up against. And I'm here to tell you with the twenty-twenty hindsight what very few are willing or able to share.

Part III
No Longer a Victim

I see her as a little girl. What a great life she had! A loving family, wonderful friends, family vacations, and visits with everyone that she loved every summer. I wonder how she made that turn down the wrong path and why she didn't see it coming. I see her dancing, smiling, laughing, and twirling around on hot summer days. I see her outside in her backyard playing Frisbee with her friends, swinging on her swing set, enjoying every moment before the hot sun would set.

I watch her growing up. She is becoming quite lovely. I see her kindness, her heart, her love for her friends and family as the cornerstone of who she is. She has talents, too. She can dance and she can sing. She loves to share them with the world. She is a bright light. She is a spark on a dim day.

I often wonder if she didn't see the warnings because her life had been so blessed. Maybe she didn't look for danger because she had never seen danger before and she simply didn't know what it would look like. Maybe, because she was always surrounded by love and goodness, she never knew that darkness and pain existed and could one day infiltrate her life.

I want to go back and tell her on that hot, sunny day that I am so sorry for her. For what I will do to her, for what will happen, for what she will become. But she wouldn't have listened because she only believes in goodness and love, and my warning would not have made sense to her. I see the sunrays bouncing off of her bright white dress, her face glowing with an early summer tan, and I want to run over and grab her and hide her from the world. She doesn't deserve this, she doesn't deserve what will happen to her.

I want to shout to her, "I didn't know. I didn't see. I didn't look out for you," but all I can do is watch her life as she gets closer to the day that she will walk into his trap. My heart breaks every time I look back and see her.

This is my daily pain as I work to travel back in time and see where we walked off the path together. This pain, this insistence that something be learned from it, that somehow the world should change because it just can't stay like this, is what brings these very first blogs to life.

I spent twenty years hiding it, four years running from it, and now the day has arrived when I force myself to face it head on. This is by far the hardest thing I have ever done in my life. To travel back in time, to see what I have done, to learn from it, to live with it, to know that I changed her, and to know that I cannot completely undo it.

I sit for days staring at the keyboard and one day something washes over me and hits me square in my heart. I decide that I am a survivor, no longer a victim. Victims don't have choices, survivors do. Victims are stuck in their circumstances and I am not. And I find a wave of strength that I did not know I even had in me, and I will myself to continue forward.

If I am to be a true survivor, then I have to tell my story from the beginning to the end, no matter what the end becomes. I sit down and explain how I became a victim of domestic abuse because I realize something on that day: I have to go back and find Susan before I can move forward and become her again. I have left bits and pieces of her scattered throughout my past, bits and pieces that he broke off and were carried into the wind like little scraps of trash. Only I know better. Each piece of her that he threw away is a treasure. I need to go back and collect them and put them back together and when I complete this, then I can become whole again. I can be the best possible version of me again. This is going to be a long journey. I take a deep breath and head for my keyboard.

What Does SODA™ Mean to You?

Do you remember the first time you ever tasted soda? I do. I was a little girl, we were on vacation near the Jersey Shore, and I asked my parents if I could have a quarter for the soda pop machine. My brother had gotten a quarter, my sister was already drinking her favorite orange soda, and I sat staring at all the mouth-watering flavors in front of me while begging for that quarter. My dad gave in and handed me one, I pushed the button for grape soda, and it was everything I thought it would be and more. It was sweet and sticky and delicious! The can was gorgeous, a bright purple with an eye-catching design and all the right colors and shapes to attract my eye. I was hooked. Grape soda became an instant hit with me, and I was interested in no other flavor. I was loyal to this one brand, this one flavor, this one design. I stuck with grape soda every chance I had because it was all I ever wanted.

But then something changed. Puberty came on and my hips began to get wider and I started to gain weight. One summer day, probably three or four years later, I asked my mom what I could do to stop these changes. "Just give up soda," she said casually, "and your clothes will fit again in no time." WHAT? Give up soda? What was she talking about? The thing that was incredible and sweet and attractive to me was now bad for me and had changed me into something different? WHAT? How could something that seemed so good for me turn out to be bad for me? I never saw it coming.

I bet you've figured out by now that we're not talking about soda, right? But let's go with it because it works and you'll see why. We face these situations in life all the time. We find out that something we love, something that we may have thought was good for us, turns out not to be. Basically, we have three choices: first, we can ignore the obvious and keep it in our lives. We understand when we make this choice that we are consciously going to turn into something that we were not when we began. This is difficult and I have a lot more to say about this, so stick with me. Second, we can cling to indecision (keep it or give it up?) and hope that something will change. Not making a decision is making a decision = deciding to do nothing is doing something. Maybe we will learn that soda is not bad for us? Maybe we can give up something else in our lives and make it work? Maybe, maybe, maybe. All the while we live the same pattern day after day, we are exhausted by our own lives because soda is still there and in the end, nothing changes. I'll come back to this, too. Finally, we can decide to give up soda, change the situation, shake everything up and run like hell towards a change. This solution always being the best and most obvious choice, it is, of course, the hardest one to make because it takes the most courage, the most planning, the most energy, and the most effort. But what comes from this is the biggest payoff.

For now, I am only talking about choices: decide to live with a problem, decide to do nothing, or change your life and leave your problem in the dust.

My name is Susan Sparks and I am a twenty-year survivor of domestic abuse. You got it: Survivor Of Domestic Abuse. I use the analogy of SODA™ because it fits. When I first had soda, it was sweet and amazing and everything I ever wanted it to be. Then things changed over time and I found out that it was hurting me and I had a decision to make. In my life, my once charming boyfriend of four years became my husband of sixteen years and slowly turned from my Prince Charming into a frog right before my eyes. Someone who had once seemed like my dream come true became my living nightmare. I went through all three decision-making processes. First, I decided to ignore the problem and thought I could live with it. Then I couldn't decide what to do. And finally, after twenty years, I mustered the courage and strength to blow the lid off that damn can and I ran for my life. It wasn't clean, it wasn't pretty, and it wasn't without injury, but I made it. I made it to the other side, and I'm here to talk about it and tell you what I did.

I'm going to share my story because I don't want it to be yours, and if it is yours, then I want to help you get to the other side and avoid the many mistakes I made. I didn't reach out for help, I didn't have a plan, and I didn't use the incredible resources that were available to me everywhere I went. I was an abuser's dream: scared, weak, and isolated. I want to give you strength. I want to let you know that you are not alone. I want you to have a plan before you decide to leave. With those three things, you can get out safely.

Remember this: STRENGTH + SUPPORT + PLAN = FREEDOM. You can do this.

———————————

Tomorrow the world will have a new acronym, "SODA"; Survivor of Domestic Abuse." I hope it sticks, I hope it makes sense, and I hope it means something to someone. Because dredging up all of this pain, this hopelessness, and these fears have to mean something to someone or why am I doing this? I never planned to tell my story and really still don't! Yet I sit here daily and type the words because I now consider it my full-time job to share my experiences in the hopes of validating yours, to collect the broken pieces of my past and mend them back together so I can walk into my own future, and to make sure that we all get out of this as soon – and as safely – as humanly possible.

1
Sticks and Stones

(WARNING SIGN OF DOMESTIC ABUSE:)
Insults, demeans, or shames you with put-downs

From where I sit today, it is a long and difficult thought process to try and understand how I got to a place in my life where I let a man break me apart from inside out until all that was left of me was tiny little fragments of the girl I had been and the woman that I was trying to become. I see so many women who stand up for themselves when someone puts them down. I see women who aren't afraid to confront someone when they see that something wrong is going on in front of them. Yet I was not one of them and, if you are reading this book, I'm guessing that you are not, either. At a time in my life when I needed me the most, I was not there. Where was I and why? Why did I have his back instead of my own? Isn't that really what it all comes down to? We serve their needs instead of our own? Of course it is.

Is this something that we blame on nature? On nurture? Or do we simply blame ourselves the rest of our lives? And why is it still so impossibly hard to fully blame him when he is the monster that was in my bed, lurking in my shadows, and waiting behind every corner to jump out and scare the life out of me? How do I sit quietly with all of the pain that he left inside me, so much pain that I am still nauseous to even write about this? Who do I blame? Who do you blame?

It's easy enough to blame nature because I was born with a quiet and sweet temperament, a people-pleaser. So, moms, dads, parents, daughters, sisters, and friends, watch out for people like us. Watch out for the sweet ones who always aim to please, who will laugh at their own expense, and who do almost anything to make everyone else happy. We are easy marks because there is something inside of us that drives us to feel that we need to save the world and we forget- or don't realize – that we may need to one day save ourselves.

It hurts terribly to think about how badly I let myself down. I betrayed myself, and I ultimately blame myself more than I blame him or anyone or anything else. All of these years later I have the most anger and the most pain about how I treated me. I deal with this even today. Even as I write, I write slowly, as if I will unravel the words and see them spill out in front of me like an untwisted ball of yarn, and suddenly it will all be still and peaceful and make sense right in front of my eyes. But it never does. How do we ever make sense of abuse?

Nurture is the one that I analyze the most. What happened to me is the opposite of what happens to victims of childhood abuse in so many cases. Victims of childhood abuse grow up and they look at the world with different eyes. They look for signs of evil and abuse so that they can either avoid it, or walk into it again, because it is what they know. Do you ever think about that? Do you ever think about why you walked into the life that you did? Of course. We all do.

For me, having had that wonderful childhood, that amazing family, I wasn't looking for anything. I was looking for a continuation of the peaceful life that I was already living. And maybe, perhaps, it has been suggested, I let a lot slide with my then boyfriend/fiancé/husband because I only knew men to be good and so expected him to be good, too. I wasn't looking for red flags because I had only seen white ones in my life. He could have shown up with one hundred red flags, and he did; but I never saw them because I didn't know to look for them.

What do we do with this? We educate ourselves, our children, our sisters, our friends, our communities, that abuse is everywhere. It happens to one in four, and it does not just happen to former victims of abuse or people who have headed down the wrong path in life. It happens to women from all walks of life, and we need to look for it. Most importantly, if you recognize yourself as a victim of abuse, let yourself off the hook; it happens to one in four. Not one in four thousand, or one in four hundred. The key is this: we need to work together to understand what to do next.

What did I miss? So much. Maybe the first time he put me down I just thought he was in a bad mood and ignored it. But maybe after he started putting me down again and again, something should have registered with me that this was not right. Why didn't it? Because I was a people- pleaser and wanted to see him happy; thus, I would not confront him. For sure, that is a reason.

And maybe because he was amazing at telling me that I was overreacting and made me feel so stupid for standing up for myself that he trained me not to. Maybe I had more fight in me in the beginning than I remember. I only remember that it felt like he was always right. That I was wrong. That he was always the winner and I the loser. That he was smarter, that he knew better. If I was clearly right and he mistaken, he brushed it off. And if I was wrong, he made a federal case out of it to be sure that I knew that I had messed up again. Sound familiar?

He made me feel shame every day. I felt shame for making mistakes that I may or may not have made. I felt shame for not being pretty enough for him when I was making a great deal of money as a model. I felt shame for not being physically fit enough for him when I got up at 5:00 a.m. and worked out seven days a week. I remember walking across the street one day when he reached over and put his hand on my rear end and said, "Why is this so mushy if you work out every day?" I was humiliated. Because I couldn't get anything right. Because I had not worked out properly. I look back now at photos and see what my body looked like. It was a body that most would kill for. It was a body that he made me feel ashamed of. His words hurt me. I let them.

I see her sitting in the middle of their living room with tears in her eyes. It is a cold and snowy night, pitch black outside. She is 25 years old and very thin. The large sofa makes her look like a tiny doll as she sits very still with her hands folded gently in her lap. She is wondering to herself what has just happened. He loved to show her off to the world. It was so weird to her. He told her at home how awful she looked but he loved to make her dress up and parade her around town like a Barbie doll. The problem was that no matter what she put on to wear he would absolutely hate it and get angry at her. He would ask her every day why she bought the ugly clothes that she bought? He said she looked like "Laura Ashley." She had no idea what that meant so she looked up Laura Ashley and found bedspreads with paisley prints and flowers.

So that year for the holidays he went out and bought her a new wardrobe that he wanted to see her wear because he was tired of her ugly clothing. Her family had come over and he was excited to bring out all of the boxes and show off what he had done. Gathered in the living room to exchange presents after dinner, everyone was having a pretty good time until he left the room to go get her stack of presents. She watched her family's faces turn to looks of horror and shock as she opened box after box of what looked like clothes that would be worn in bad porn flicks. Her family was clearly upset, bewildered, and each made excuses to get out of there the second she was done opening the stack of boxes. Piece after piece of cheap, awful clothing sat piled on the sofa next to her and she couldn't turn her head to look at it; she felt as if she had just been asked to take off all of her own clothing in front of her family. She felt humiliated to her core.

"Well," he demands, "Do you like it?" "Yes," she mutters quietly, to keep the peace. Once again, she is trapped in a no-win situation.

"You hate all of it, don't you!" he yells in her face. "You're so ungrateful! I did all of this shopping and you don't like anything? What's the matter with these clothes? You would finally look good when we went out! Well then I'm taking it all back!" He storms out of the room in rage as she sits on the sofa feeling like the loneliest person in the world. She has just been tortured, embarrassed, and abused in front of her family with holiday gifts. Then she is yelled at for not liking them. And now she is sitting here trying to figure out how to make everyone happy again. She feels a tear slide down her face. What in the world was going on here?

It's memories like these that force me to look back and try to understand how we let that happen. How we let them get so important? Them so strong and us so weak? What kept me from storming out that night and not turning back? The thought never even occurred to me. I was four years into our relationship. We were in love but not yet married. The thought of children had not yet even entered my mind. There was nothing in the world holding me back, so what was keeping me there? That line from The Eagles song comes to mind, "So often times it happens that we live our lives in chains and we never even know we have the key."

―――――――

I see her as a child in grade school. She is sitting at her desk waiting to begin her creative writing project and she is excited! She couldn't fall asleep the night before as the words and images were flashing through her mind and the story that she wanted to write for her project was starting to form. Oh, how she loved writing!

She sees her friends chewing on their pencils, squirming in their seats, fretting about what they will write about. But she is like a race car revving at the starting line. She is just waiting to hear the word "Go!" and she will take off at high speed. Writing had always been this way for her. She would see the images, then she would simply put her pencil on the paper and the story would flow out. It's like she went into a trance. She didn't think, she didn't choose her words, they just flowed out of her like a song flows out of a singer or music flows from the fingertips of a prodigy playing the piano. It just happened, and it made her feel alive.

She is in fourth grade, a very popular girl with lots of friends. She has a sunny disposition and loves to make others laugh. She is serious about her schoolwork but fully embraces life and play at all other times. She sees her life as a series of fun adventures awaiting her at every turn. She fears nothing because life has not taught her to be afraid. She is full of love and joy. She has the security of her family to go home to every day, and that is all the foundation that she needs. Her whole life stretches out in front of her like a giant rainbow with all the colors to choose from, all the magic to experience, and every word she can possibly see for her story as it flows from her mind onto her paper. She can't wait to see what will happen next.

She maintains her love of words as she grows through the years. She enters college and knows that she will choose a career that somehow relates to writing. She falls in love with journalism and takes every print and broadcast class that she can find in order to keep writing and telling stories. This is her passion come to life, and she can't believe that she could actually get paid to do this one day!

She is eighteen now and a force to be reckoned with. She is bright, smart, strong, and ready to take on the world. She is a leader, yet still kind and caring to those around her. She has many friends, and she continues to both work and play hard. She has matured, but she is still the same person that she was as she sat at that fourth-grade desk. She is full of life, and hers is stretched out in front of her like that rainbow has somehow flattened and invited her to walk down the most colorful path ever created. Each color beckons her to new opportunities, new horizons, and colorful and glowing stories that will result from her experiences.

She flows through her college years with ease and determination at the same time. She socializes and makes a whole new group of friends at school that become like a second family to her as they all travel the journey together. She is popular, she is at the top of her class, and life is hers for the taking as she prepares to enter her senior year in college.

She lives off-campus in an apartment building like many of the upperclassman do during their final year at school. She is independent and running her own life now. She is making her own choices, managing work, school, and play, and she has everything right where she wants it to be.

I see her go to the gym that sultry August night. She is dressed in pink workout clothes and her long hair is pulled back into a ponytail. She walks in and looks for an available exercise bike. She finds one, climbs on, puts on her earphones and starts her workout tape. She sets the bike timer for forty-five minutes and begins her routine.

She doesn't notice, but he sees her immediately. He is lifting weights. He watches her every move and is surveying her intently. He hasn't seen her here before, and he is immediately curious about who she is, where she came from, and why he doesn't know her. He wants to know her.

Then she looks up and she sees him, too. He is staring right at her. She catches her breath, he is so handsome! She tries to keep her eyes off of him as she rides the bike, but she can feel his eyes on her body and it feels like they never leave her. A thrill runs over her like she has never felt before and she knows that she must meet this man. She is attracted to him, she is drawn to him, she is excited by him. She knows that her life has just somehow changed forever. She just doesn't know what it means yet.

Her timer rings and she almost falls off the bike; she is so lost in thought that it startles her! She slowly climbs down, feeling his eyes on her the whole time. She saunters by him but doesn't say a word. Nor does he. He never takes his eyes off of her as she exits the gym.

She is young, innocent, and pure. It takes him very little time to track her down and they meet. She is just 21 years old. He is 35. She, just entering her senior year of college. He, a college graduate, a working man, so worldly, so knowledgeable, she is impressed with everything about him. He is exciting and different from anyone she has ever met. If something breaks, he knows how to fix it. If something goes wrong, he knows exactly who to call. She is still finding her way, still forming her own ideas, testing life out to see how it works. He has it all together. She is drawn to him like a magnet. She has no idea that she has climbed directly into the neat and tidy spider web that he has expertly crafted for her and that her life will never be the same. He will charm her with his knowledge of the world. He will charm her with his manners, his friends, his fancy car, and his big apartment. He will tell her that he knows celebrities, has ties in important places, can take her to all of the fancy restaurants in town. He will be larger than life. And for her, with her life just beginning, he is magical. She sees nothing more than the spell he has cast, and she won't see any differently until it is far, far too late and she is simply stuck in the center of the web.

This one night is one of the hardest to think back to. "What if" always running through my mind. But I am a firm believer in fate, and somehow this man was to be my fate whether I asked for it or not. If I could go back and tell her not to go to the gym that night I now know it would make no difference because he would meet me the next day at the grocery store, or local restaurant, or wherever our paths were destined to cross. It was our fate for the colorful butterfly to gently rest in the sticky lair of the man who was to become my husband.

For so many years now my words were lost. My beautiful words that I would see and would then flow to paper directly from my brain as if I was writing my own symphony. But on this day, something strikes me, and I rush to my keyboard. This day I type, slowly at first with lots of deep breaths, about a subject that still pains my heart. How he took words, my favorite things in the world, and used them against me. How he took love, my favorite feeling in the world, and used it against me. How he took living, the thing I did so effortlessly, and made me stop doing it.

Writing this one hurts much more than the others in so many ways, but I force myself to do it because without it I cannot keep walking through to the other side of the journey that we have started. And I need something back that I cannot live without. I need my words.

Sticks and Stones...

...will break our bones but words will never hurt us? Whoever originally said that knew NOTHING about domestic abuse. We face them every day in the world of domestic abuse, words that hurt us beyond repair. We find ourselves trapped in situations that somehow have gotten bigger than we are.

It didn't start that way. It started as dating, or love, or marriage. But somehow along the way it changed into something dark and scary, and when we want to leave we feel trapped by something that is bigger than we are. Walk away? It's never that easy. What's keeping us there? Words? Well, yeah.

If you ever meet a SODA™ I hope you never ask them any questions about what made them stay, why they stayed so long, or why they finally left. We don't need you to ask these questions. We ask ourselves every day, and it is our job and our job only, to discover the answers and make peace with them when we are on the other side and when we are ready. Words kept you there? How does that work? Was he holding sticks and stones? No. Was he hurling really scary words at you that made you fear for your life? Yep.

We deal with these questions on our own at night when we can't sleep. We deal with them in every new relationship that we form, and we deal with them in the work we do through therapy or counseling or whatever help we choose to seek. We choose. Words swirl all around us like titles on a resume that we now own forever. They become tattoos on our souls and we are forever branded: survivor, victim, weak, strong.

Words are a powerful thing in the world of domestic abuse. Remember, it is words that started our problems in the first place. "I love you," turns to "Who would love you?" "You look pretty tonight" turns to "You're lucky to have me because no one else would ever think you're pretty." It's endless, and endless is bigger than we are.

And what happens when you find the courage and the strength to leave? I can tell you what happened to me. "You're a great mom" turned to "You're a horrible mom." "You can always trust her" turned to "She's crazy and a liar, don't trust a word she says." His words were so convincing because he was so good with them. He practiced his craft every day and many believed him. I did.

Abuse will be here as long as human beings are on this Earth. So will cruel words. The titles we choose to take away and keep with us are entirely up to us, whether we are living with our abuser, still forced to be in contact with our abuser, or only hear their voice in our heads on those dark nights that we can't sleep.

I have cast aside "victim" and I have chosen "survivor"; that is something that I strive to be every day in my new life. That is something that he never called me. I work hard on this as I walk the path of recovery from abuse, leave that life behind, and stare something down that is no longer bigger than me.

So ironic is my life that I am a writer! Words are some of my favorite things in the world. So, if I get to use words, then I get to use words any way I want. I am here to turn the ugliness that words can have upside down on its head and make them magical again. I want to use words to heal, not to harm. I want to use words to change a life, not hurt one. Words are now my tool of choice, not sticks nor stones, because I can use words for power, too, and it looks like I just took my power back.

If you are truly to be free, then you get to choose your words, too. And you get to choose when something is no longer bigger than you are. "Powerful?" "Strong?" "Ready?" "Fearless?" What do you want to be called today?

Remember this: STRENGTH + SUPPORT + PLAN = FREEDOM. You can do this.

It's taken almost four years for me to get my words back. Not just to be able to type them, but to be able to speak them, too. To say, "I am a survivor." To admit that I suffered and not just be able to say it, but to allow myself to feel something again without the unmanageable fear that feeling will be my undoing. To tell a story is simple, but to feel the old and way-too-familiar pain as we tell the story, well that is asking a lot from a victim of abuse. How much are we supposed to suffer before we can say it is over? Where is the end, and how do we know when we have gotten there?

Those of us who fall into the trap of an abuser often become a curiosity. Everyone wants to know how it happened. How did such a bright light fall in love with someone determined to pull her plug? Everyone wants to read the cautionary tale to make sure that they don't become the next victim.

Everyone who has fallen into the same trap wants to know that they did not fall alone. Indeed, we fell together, and that is why I do this every day. I break, I heal, and I break again to assure all of us that we have fallen together and indeed we will rise together.

Today I publish this blog. The writing of it has brought me back to the pain I endured. It reopens the wounds. But if it makes one person stop asking me, or you, or someone else who has suffered domestic abuse why we stayed, then it was worth the heartbreak of writing it. If it reassures one person still in the midst of an abusive situation that she is not alone, it was worth it. And if it compels someone to leave an abusive relationship, I would gladly suffer it again and again.

Why did we stay? We stayed because we were scared. We stayed because we got trapped. We stayed because they said they would change and we loved them and we believed them. We stayed because we were born this way. We stayed because no one warned us. We stayed because their behavior toward us was beyond our ability to understand. We stayed because we believed we should.

You don't understand us unless you are one of us so you'll have to take our word for it. So, to help us please don't ask this question. Simply learn, support, or help. And if it's you, please know that it will not change and get yourself out with a solid plan to end your cycle of abuse. Don't stay one day longer than you need to. I did. I stayed too long.

2

Everybody Wants to Rule Your World

(WARNING SIGN OF DOMESTIC ABUSE:
Prevents you from making your own decisions)

It is not a typical situation for the abuse victim to be the one who makes the most money in their marriage. But it does happen, and it happened in my case. And maybe that is why he fought so much harder to control me over the years. During the day I was a powerful executive. I ran a huge part of a huge company. I would direct my employees, I would run large projects, I would manage budgets in the millions of dollars. I would speak in front of thousands of people. I was a true powerhouse, and I commanded respect for what I did.

At night I would come home and he would already be there. He was there because he had stopped working a day job and started taking on dream projects that were fun for him but never ended up making any money. He stopped working when he learned just how much money I was making and understood that he did not have to work any longer because I could support us both. You would think that would put someone in a great mood! But he wasn't. Ever. I would come home and hear, "Is that what you wore to work today?" or "Are you really getting home this late?" or "Why don't we ever have any groceries in this house? Are you serious? Do you have so many problems that you can't go to the grocery store?"

As I walked in the door he would be barking about what he had decided I had done wrong that day. And after 8 – 12 hours at work, I was not prepared to deal with him. I had learned that it was easier to just agree and apologize and tell him that I would take care of it that weekend – whatever it might be – than to fight back. This was the beginning of me entering the peacekeeping phase, doing anything to keep him calm so I could escape his fury. I knew by now that if I tried to walk away he would follow; fight back and he would escalate; deny and he would rage. What other choice did I have than to agree?

Interpreting my peaceful approach as weakness, he worked harder and harder to control my actions. And he worked really hard at this. He once said to me, "If you put yourself up on a pedestal it will be my job to knock you off. You are conceited and full of yourself and you make me sick." He said those words to me over twenty years ago, words that felt like a kick to the stomach, and I've never forgotten them. I had been raised to believe that a man who loved you was supposed to put you up on a pedestal; he thought his job was to knock me off of one if I accidentally got excited about myself and stepped up there? I was so sad. My partner was not a partner at all. My mate was more like a shark, me a guppy, us in a barrel. The sadness was overwhelming. Every time I saw one of my friends' men compliment them, I felt like someone had stabbed me in the heart. Every time I saw a romantic comedy on

TV, I turned the channel before I could see the joy in their eyes. It was too much for me to take. I was with someone whose ultimate mission was to diminish me.

With my despair came a whole new level of weakness which was perfect for him because he wanted to control what I did all of the time. The higher I climbed at work, the more he dug his talons into me at home. It was horrible. He wanted to choose my friends. He wanted to say ok to where I went before I went there. He wanted to control my appearance. He told me when I needed to lose weight. He picked what we watched on TV, where we went on vacation, where we went to dinner, and mocked my choices for TV shows, restaurants, and vacation spots when I tried to assert myself. He said I watched what idiots watched, ate where low class people ate, and vacationed where losers went. It became a losing battle. I often wonder when I stopped feeling the intense emotional pain and started slowly going numb. It doesn't mean that I didn't feel pain every single time he lashed out at me, it simply means that I had to learn to adapt to his behavior in order to survive. The question becomes: How much pain can we endure before our brains start blocking out some of it and allowing us to react on autopilot?

In retrospect, the problem was that I was just seeing each little battle for what it was. A battle. A little issue that would go away because he was, after all, the man I was in love with; and when you loved a man he was inherently a good person, right? I mean my dad was my role model, and he was a great man, so this man would be a great man, too. I never saw that I was entering a war. I never saw the bigger picture because I was stuck in the weeds of battle. I didn't know that issues would turn into topics and topics would turn into conversations and conversations would turn into lectures and lectures would turn into battles, and battle after battle after battle and you have yourself a war. Oh, what a war you have.

———————

I see her getting ready for their date that night. She wants to look so pretty for him. She sits at her desk and pulls her long hair back and makes spiral curls that hang loosely around her face. It was a long day at school and she wants to look fresh and lovely for him. She pulls out a beautiful top and sexy jeans and heels and knows that she looks ready for a wonderful night. She races to finish her reading for her college classes tomorrow and is ready and waiting when he knocks on her door. She flings it open with a big smile on her face and he stands there taking her in. He looks like something is wrong but doesn't say anything. He asks if she is ready and they leave.

I see them walk down the hall together toward the elevator. She looks absolutely stunning and heads turn as they enter the corridor to the lobby. Heads will turn again when they enter the restaurant, but she won't see them. She is a bright light in a darkened moment, but she doesn't know it yet; infatuated, she's focused only on him, waiting to see what he says and does next. He is becoming important to her and she wants to see him happy. His reaction is the only one that matters to her.

At dinner, he leans across the table and brushes a curl off her face. "Why do you wear your hair like this?" he asks. "Why?" she says. "I wear my hair differently almost every day. It's why I love my long hair. Sometimes it's up, sometimes it's down." "No," he says, "Not good. That's unsettling. You look different. You don't even look like the person I took out last week, you look like someone else. It doesn't look good this way. You look like a little girl with curly hair and too much makeup. Silly. Don't do that again. Your hair only looks good down. You should only wear it that way."

She sits there embarrassed and feeling foolish. She's out with this attractive older man and he has just said that she looks like a little girl. She feels so dumb. She needs to wear her hair down from now on or he will not take her out again. She decides that she will do that, it's no big deal anyway and that's what he wants. It is her first concession.

"And what's with this sweater?" he asks. "What?" she says now visibly upset. "Who wears a sweater on a date? How is that even attractive?" "Oh," she leans back against the booth thinking how badly she has blown this night. *I can't believe what a mess I am* she silently thinks to herself. "You know what really looks good, don't you? You need to wear solid color tops and dark blue jeans. Haven't you seen what the other girls are wearing? You know those brown boots that go to your knees? That looks really good."

"Oh?" she says with a glimmer of hope. *Maybe he is going to give her a second chance.*

But the second chances were always given after she was told what she did wrong the first time, and boy did she always get it wrong the first time. And what she did wrong the first time always had to be changed, corrected, and controlled by him. Her clothes, her hair, her makeup, were just the beginning. He was slowly breaking her in and wearing her down, about to strip her bare. Not just for an outward makeover, but straight down to her soul. A makeover of her complete being that she never asked for and never expected.

As I write this blog I realize the memories are still raw, and I have muttered a few choice words at the pain and anguish, the anger and degradation I suffered for so many years as he silently ruled my world and made every day hurt. I couldn't come down the stairs without being insulted. I couldn't enter a room without hearing a critical comment. Even if I followed his rules I could never get it right, I could and would, never win. It was his game.

Everybody Wants to Rule Your World...

There's a famous song by the band Tears for Fears from the 1980s. It says, "Welcome to your life. There's no turning back." I heard it the other day and it absolutely struck me to a place where I stood still and only listened to their words. They are so true.

How many days do we relive our lives in our minds wishing they had gone differently? How many times do we ask ourselves, "How did this happen?" or "How did I end up here?" What if I told you that it doesn't matter? What if I told you that you could figure that out later and that the only thing that really matters is today and what you do NEXT?

As domestic abuse victims, we spend a lot of time beating ourselves up for our mistakes and blaming ourselves for how we got here. We don't always need our abusers to tell us what is wrong with us. They do such a great job that when they leave the room we often just pick up where they left off and we repeat the same things in our own minds. We look at our lives and we think, "What have I done?" And doing that is so wrong. It leaves us feeling so despondent, filled with such despair. We are making ourselves even weaker. Who can bounce back from that?

Well, here's a thought. I've never seen a time machine. So, you can't go back. You can't un-meet someone, you can't un-date someone, you can't un-fall in love with someone, and you can't un-marry them (divorce does not equal un-marrying someone. Divorce means to end a marriage that you already started). You are where you are and that is here, today. You know what you have to do next? Think about this: if you only had today, and today was the only day that mattered in your entire life, and you had to rate it on a scale of 1-10 where would you rank it? How many days are you living like this every week?

Do you know what the song goes on to say? It says, "Everybody wants to rule the world." You know what I sing when I hear the song now? I sing, "Everybody wants to rule MY WORLD." If you're a SODA™ and still living in a life of domestic abuse then you know exactly what I am talking about. They want to rule your world. You have lost control and you no longer feel like you have any say in your own life. But guess what? THE CONTROL IS YOURS TO TAKE BACK.

Who brought you to this day in your life? You did. Who met, dated, loved, married, moved in with, whatever you did, to get you where you are today? You did. So, who can move you to the next step? You can. Only you can. There is only one person who can decide what your next step is, and that is you. YOU RULE YOUR WORLD. Say it in your mind whether you believe it or not: I RULE MY WORLD. How strong do you feel right now? It was always yours but now you know for sure. IT IS YOURS. I promise you this, it is yours.

If you have only today, what do you want to do with it? Do you want tomorrow to be another today or do you want tomorrow to be a day that you can remember forever as the day that you decided to rule your own world?

The song ends by saying, "So glad we've almost made it..." Well, have we? Not yet. One in four women will experience domestic abuse in her lifetime, so there is work to be done. Only you control you, so you can help change that statistic when you are ready to change your life. Every day I get up and rule my world. Is life easy? Not always. Is life better? YES! Fun? YES! Am I in control of my own actions, my own decisions, my own movements, and my own choices? OH, HELL YES. It's never too late. It took me twenty years to get my feet under me and get out that door. If you are not there yet, don't feel bad. Use me as an example; I was trapped inside that soda can for a long time. It was dark and cold and scary and I felt completely isolated and alone in there. I felt powerless and broken. I felt weak and unable to move. I'm telling you that one in four of us are living this life right now, today, and I'm telling you that only you should rule your world.

Remember this: STRENGTH + SUPPORT + PLAN = FREEDOM. You can do this.

———————————

I sit at the keyboard with a knot in my stomach. To think of how much control he had over me. To think of the power I gave away. To relive this in writing these blogs is almost more than I can take. But I think of the stories I have yet to tell you, I think of the advice I have yet to give and I cringe, but I move forward. Brace yourself, I'll brace myself. This is going to be a tough ride. The payoff? Freedom. Let it ring.

———————————

I see her at age 22. They have been dating a year now. I see how he is still setting the trap for her. He is most often mellow and sweet when he is around her, yet sometimes slips and loses his temper with others. She does not consider this her issue. She is twenty-two, and twenty-two year olds only think about themselves. Twenty-two year olds think they are immortal and impervious to the variations of the world. Twenty-two year olds are naïve.

I see them come together at the end of the day each day. He welcomes her with open arms and a gentle hug. He makes her feel warm and safe and protected. She is blossoming in the light of his love. She does not yet know who she is dating.

I see them at the grocery store one Sunday afternoon. She has lost her grocery list, then found it, then somehow dropped it out of the grocery cart. She is tired from a long week at work and she is frustrating herself. He is walking easily next to her watching her bumble along and gently laughing at her. He just keeps putting his items in the cart without saying a word. She realizes that it is taking them twice as long to shop because she is dropping her list and forgetting what she needs and she keeps doubling back to get things she has forgotten. "How annoyed are you?" she asks humbly as she looks for her list yet again. "Annoyed?" he smiles, "I'm not annoyed. Let's just get what we need and we'll be set." She feels an overwhelming sense of gratitude for this kind and patient man.

As they put their groceries into his car she feels the warmth spread over her again, "Do you know what I like the best about you?" she asks with a heart full of love and sincerity.

"What?" he looks intently into her eyes to search for the answer before she can reveal it.

"I love that you have no temper. You have no temper at all!" she smiles back at him. "I mean that's amazing. No matter what I do, or what happens around us, you just don't get angry or upset. You're so calm and so sweet. You have no temper. I just love that about you."

"That's true," he remarks with a smile, "There's no reason to get upset. What purpose would it serve anyway?"

When I think about the self-control and discipline that it took this man to hide his true self from me for four years, to keep his anger, his fury, the flames that burn inside of him smashed so far beneath the surface that I could not smell his burning flesh, I marvel. I marvel at him, I marvel at his masterful performance, I marvel at the extent he would and could go to in order to hide his true self from me until he knew he "had me" after we were married.

And it's for this reason, this incredibly legitimate reason, that I just can't beat myself up over and over again about how I got into that situation. Because it is a very common pattern for abusers to hide their true selves and their behaviors from their victims until they groom their victims into falling in love with them. We all need to recognize and understand this. We can't blame ourselves for stepping into a trap that we did not see.

I was the woman he wanted. I was the world he wanted to rule. He was willing to go to great lengths to achieve that goal. He had the self-control and discipline to present himself, at first, as a person without a temper and with the patience of a saint. Maybe those were two major red flags right there for me. Even my father, my role model and foundation in life, had both a temper and a limit to his patience. I saw it all the time. He hid it from no one because he was human like the rest of us. But this man did. He hid it from me until it was too late and I had fallen in love with an illusion. I was young and naïve. Love is blind. A deadly combination.

It is a test of my spirit, it is a test of my strength, and it is a testament to all of us who know the life of domestic abuse, that he never broke me. He never will. But damn, he got so close.

3
You Are What You Do

It's very tough when I look back to see how this spanned two decades. I lost twenty years of my life the same way someone who goes to prison loses twenty years of their life, freedom, and the ability to make their own daily choices. I can see now that there were warning signs. But I can also see how I fell in love with a man who hid his true identity from me when I was a young girl. I can see how I stayed hoping it would get better. But when I look back and I see those hours turn into days and those days turn into years and those years turn into decades, that thought is staggering. How do we let this happen? Simultaneously explainable and indescribable, it is the life of the victim of domestic abuse.

I see her at age 36 standing in the kitchen of their large home. She is dressed in a designer outfit and looks like she has just stepped off the cover of a magazine. It is a Sunday morning and she is waiting for all of her friends and family to arrive. He has kept her from seeing them in one way or another for a few months now, and she has finally convinced him to let her throw a brunch so she can see everyone at once. He had ignored her request the first few times, but she had been persistent this time and would not let it go. Finally, he had agreed and told her that she would have to do everything: decorate, cook, set up, clean up, and be sure to include everyone that he wanted, too. She was happy to agree; anything to see her friends and family that she so desperately missed. She should have been somehow tipped off that this was going too smoothly, but she was so excited to see everyone that she got busy with planning menus and ordering food and buying pretty plates and napkins and picking out her new outfit to wear.

All of this being a recipe for disaster of course: spending money, being happy, and focusing on herself and not him. But she missed it, missed the warning signs. As the days got closer to that Sunday he was becoming tenser and lashing out at her more than usual. But she was keeping herself busy with the details of the party and trying to stay away from him as much as possible. She was going to see her family and all of her friends at once. That was better than her birthday! He hated her birthday. This was just going to be a great day for no reason and she was so excited.

The morning of the brunch, everything was set up to perfection. People started showing up right at 10:00 a.m., and they immediately started laughing and reconnecting and having a wonderful time together. Yet every time she looks up at him he is either staring at her or scowling at her. She feels a familiar knot start to form in her stomach, and she knows that something is about to go badly.

By pure instinct she sticks close to her brother. They grab a plate of food and sit together and happily munch away, sharing funny stories. Just having him by her side gives her peace, and she starts to relax. They have a full house and everyone is having a great time. Laughter abounds, the food is delicious, and you can look around and see that people are really enjoying themselves.

Then she hears his voice above the noise of the crowd, and the room suddenly gets quiet. She's not sure that she's heard what she thinks she's heard, but everyone is looking at her, so she stops talking to her brother and she listens in. She hears it again and now she's sure. She hears him say, very loudly, "Susan's vagina..."

She and her brother lock eyes and his face goes very pale. She hears a few forced laughs and a few embarrassed coughs and the room is suddenly silent. Now, knowing he has full command, he continues, smile bright. "Yeah, I said to the doctor, while you're in there fixing her hernia, why don't you add a few stitches to Susan's vagina and put her back like she used to be?"

Her brother looks like he is going to throw up and he quietly gets up from the table and leaves the room. People scatter in all directions, grabbing more food, starting forced conversations, doing whatever they can to make this horrible moment pass, and she sits there at the kitchen table stuck in a moment where she can do nothing but feel the surge of humiliation, pain, embarrassment, and pure white anger flood through her body like an IV full of fire and ice water.

She wills herself to have no facial expression. She asks herself if she wants to laugh, smirk, react or not react. All of this happens in a millisecond. She feels like she is going to throw up the last bite of food that she ate. She feels it coming back on her and she wills it to stay wherever it is, trapped somewhere between her mouth and her stomach, not knowing if she's pushed the up or the down button on that elevator.

She sees all the faces turn into one as they blur. She begs her eyes not to continue to fill with tears. That would be the ultimate betrayal to herself right now, and she won't let it happen. She doesn't want to leave the room because she knows that she will fall apart and cry and not come back. She has to do something and she has no answer but to sit there, stare down at her plate, and not move.

Then she sees her brother out of the corner of her eye. He had not left the room but is standing at the trash can dumping his plate of food. Clearly his appetite is now gone. He needed to move in that moment, do something, and so had gotten up and moved away to gain his composure. He comes back to the table and sits down next to her. She looks up at him and the pain in his eyes is more than she can bear, but she won't look away. He's the only one brave enough to come near her right now.

"I think it's time I took my family home," he says sadly. She stands up to help him find his wife and children, and she's grateful to have a reason to move, to do something, to become the hostess again and start functioning. They say nothing to one another as they find everyone and gather their belongings. She asks them if they want to take some food home; they do not. It is obvious that they want to get out of there as quickly as possible, and she does not blame them. She knows that her brother is doing everything possible not to go over and punch him, and she feels her heart breaking again. Just another time he has broken her heart. Just another time he has upset her family. Just another time. She knows that her brother is feeling every emotion that she is feeling and thinking all the same thoughts. Why is she still here? Why is she putting up with this? She is so sad, so embarrassed, and there is no apology great enough to heal the moment for either one of them. She hugs him and says a soft goodbye and wonders when she will see her brother again.

Later that night she thinks about how and when this all started and why she didn't see it coming? It had been bad, but never as bad as what he had just done to her. He didn't care about the audience that he had just alienated because they were mostly her family and friends and it was his goal to never see them with her again. He was never concerned about losing his friends because he only had one or two, and for some ungodly reason they stuck by his side no matter what. They were blind to his cruelty, always on his side, and as ignorant about human kindness as he was. He had nothing to lose by acting this way, and knew that she did. So, he went to town and stoned her in front of everyone. This was not the first time that he had done this to her, and it would not be the last. This she knew all too well by this point. This had started as early as when they had first met. This one huge warning sign, his trying to isolate her from her family and friends. But she didn't know to look out for it, she didn't know it was a sign, and so she had simply let it pass her by.

———————

She sees the look of anger on her best friend's face as she tells her that she is going to miss her birthday party downtown that night. "What?" she almost yells in her face. "What are you talking about? This has been planned for months! I'm turning twenty-one! We can drink! Everyone is coming! How could you not come?"

How could she not come? The words shoot through her head like a bullet as she searches for an explanation, any explanation that could somehow make this ok, but she can't find one. *He doesn't want me to go* she thinks to herself. She can't tell her friend that; she can't even begin to think about saying that out loud when she can't even make sense of it in her own head.

She can still see his face, full of disgust as he asks her, "Are you really going to that little party tonight?"

Everything was "little" with him when he wanted to make it seem unimportant. "How did you do on your little test?" The little test being her exam that would equate to half of her grade that semester. What's up with your "little project," or your "little family reunion?" It was always little to him to make sure that she knew that it had better not interfere with her having time for him. Because he was big. He came first and everything else was little.

"I have a huge exam tomorrow, we're traveling, I have to prepare," she stumbles out lamely. She thinks stringing things together will make it sound more important like a complicated excuse instead of one stupid thing that her friend could argue with. She's gotten better at this lately as it seems that lately she is making more and more excuses for not being where people expect her to be.

"Wow," says her friend, "Ever since you met him you seem to show up less and less." She's stunned at the words of her best friend and she stands there motionless. Her friend has said what she knows everyone has been thinking for months now, but no one was quite ready to say out loud. She knew that she was pulling the oldest and dumbest trick in the book and now she was finally being called out on it: she was putting the new boyfriend in front of her dearest friends, and her friend was right.

But, unlike when she had done this in high school because she was young and dumb and didn't know any better, this time she felt like she had no real choice. In high school, she put that guy first because she was selfish and just wanted to be with him and assumed her friends would understand. They didn't. And they were right. Boyfriends would come and go, friends were forever. Now, here she was doing it again?

But her friend didn't know what was going on at home. She was being told she could not be around them, he didn't like them, they were too young, they were immature, they were bringing her down, and "she was too good for them." He was systematically severing her ties to them with the invisible hatchet that was his manipulation. He was making the choice for her because she wouldn't stand up and make him put down his weapon.

"I'm sorry," she says sadly, searching her friend's face for any sign that the relationship might survive. They had four years of friendship through college and so many amazing times together. They had grown up so much since they had first met and become close. They took classes together, had lunch together, and went out together every single weekend. They studied hard and they partied hard. And they always came out on top. They had the world in the palms of their hands until she let it slip away. And there it went again. There went another piece of her world.

She sees anger and coldness staring back at her directly from the eyes of her very best friend. It was too much, and her friend wouldn't take anymore. She wouldn't allow herself to be hurt any longer. She couldn't be disappointed again and again and again. Now she was bailing on her best friend's twenty-first birthday party? She nods and silently walks away in defeat. She knows it's the last time they'll ever talk, and she's right.

This whole situation taps into a deep-seated insecurity within her that she will somehow end up alone. And while she has the confidence to know that she can easily make friends, she's not willing to risk losing a boyfriend, much less a potential husband, to put her friends first. She's not sure why she's so afraid of being alone, without a man, but every part of her surges toward a future with a partner by her side as if she somehow cannot trust herself to forge her own path. The truth of this matter is so ironic. She was one of those girls who had always been at the top. Top of her class, top of the competitions, lots of friends, great family. So, what made her so afraid to face the world on her own? And what's the worst part? We so often choose to face the world with someone by our side who is going to make our lives so much harder than what they would have been if we had simply faced them alone to begin with.

She hates facing this truth. What made her so weak inside that she didn't know how to stand up for herself and just be where she wanted to be when she wanted to be there? She reflects back on her high school days and it's a little easier to understand. She made a classic rookie mistake. She fell in love with her first boyfriend, had stars in her eyes, thought he was her forever, and put him first. He was a kind-hearted person and never asked her not to see her friends or to ignore them. She just consistently chose him first until her friends ran out of patience with her. But so many young girls do this. The question is: Why do we still do so when we are old enough to know better? She struggled with this.

In high school, she had this deep-seated need for her first boyfriend's love and for his attention, and she craved it so much that she couldn't get enough. Was this what other girls did? She honestly didn't know. She just knew that there were never enough hours in the day, never enough days in the week for her to be with him, and her friends became less and less important. By the time she and her high school boyfriend broke up during her college years, her high school friends had all scattered to colleges of their own. She reached out to many to try and make amends, and while some reacted with kindness and were happy to hear from her, those who had been closest to her and hurt the most simply chose not to respond, and she couldn't blame them.

Then during her college years, she had started from scratch and built a whole new crew of friends. She knew what it was like to start with nothing and slowly build bonds of trust and caring that could, potentially, be with her for the rest of her life. And what was she standing here doing tonight? She was doing the exact thing over again. She was disappointing these really great girls, one by one, over and over, until she knew what would happen. She knew that they would lose patience with her and give up. This time it wasn't a classic rookie mistake. This time she was doing it like a pro. This time she was doing it with a coach behind her calling her every play directly from his pre-planned playbook. And this time she knew what the result would be.

She didn't want to look in the mirror that night when she got home because she wasn't sure that she would recognize who would be staring back at her. Who was this new person that was so afraid of losing him that she would risk losing her friends this time, knowing what would happen? And who was this girl that was so insecure about keeping him that she would change her looks, her clothing, and her hair, to make him happy? Who was she in this whole tangled-up mess? She really didn't know anymore. She had started out with all the confidence in the world. When had the world shifted so much under her feet that she would let a man tell her who she was and who she was not and where she was going to be the night of her best friend's 21st birthday party?

What she didn't want to admit to herself was that in a really odd way she was secretly relieved that she no longer had to defend her choice to her friend, or to have to face hours of questioning from him about why she hung out with her in the first place. Her actions created a decision that night for her. It wasn't a decision she would have made on her own, but it was one that would immediately make her life easier as he would be so pleased that her best friend was gone and he would have more time with her as a result. He was beginning to control her world through isolation and she was standing right next to him letting it happen because her fear of losing him was greater than the strength she had to stand up to him.

That night she lost her two best friends. When they realized she was not going to attend the birthday party, they collectively decided to write her off. They'd had it with her, and rightfully so. She was no longer a good friend to either of them. Her two friends moved in together, and the three of them never talked again. She lost. They lost.

But he won and that's all that mattered. He spent weeks telling her how much better off she was without them in her life, and at first, she was relieved to have taken care of these relationships that so annoyed him. But then holidays came around, special events they used to celebrate together, and she really started to miss them. At graduation, she felt lonely and sad as she watched them walk down the aisle and hug one another. She should have been there by their sides. She should have been in that hug. She was standing there without them. She was standing there alone.

I never blamed him for my losing them. I blamed me. I could have still been a friend, I could have still shown up. I could have defied him and done what I wanted to do. But it was easier to do what he wanted me to do and not rock the boat.

I spent years missing them and grieving over losing them. This was his first victory in separating me from my friends. I didn't see it for what it was at the time. I didn't see it for what it was until decades later. His first in what would be so many winning rounds.

So many trophies on his shelf over the years as he knocked out my friends, my family members, my neighbors, and my acquaintances. So many trophies, too many to count.

I remember how he systematically tried to break me apart from my family and I look back in sadness at what we all endured. My sister and I were best friends, and he immediately started in about how he didn't want to be around me when I was with her. "You act so different around her," he would tell me, "You act like a little child. You are so immature, you show your age. You two act like little girls." There was that word little again. We were "little girls." I think the best thing about my sister and me is that we did act like little girls. We did, after all, grow up side-by-side and somehow, through even the toughest of times in our lives, we found a way to go back and find our childlike glee and look at the world through those eyes when we were together. My sister was my best friend. His hurling of insults towards me, towards her, towards us was very painful, and he knew it. And because he knew this, he took extra pleasure in putting her down in any way that he could and at every opportunity that he could find. And because I knew he was going to do this every time we were together I did exactly what he wanted me to do; I avoided any situation where the three of us would be together. His plan was working.

He saw our incredible bond and he was immediately threatened by it. He made me feel guilty for wanting to be with her, and he made it difficult for me when I chose to be with her. There were many times that I chose him over her, and I regret every one of them. In the end, he was never successful at breaking us apart, and that is a testament to the bond that we always had and still have today. He just made us stronger. But not before we both suffered endless tests of our will to love one another, to not be broken, and to remember who we were before he came along. He pushed us to our very limits but we managed to hang on.

It was very much like this with my mom and me as well. He worked very hard to convince me she was dragging me down and setting me back in life. He didn't want her around our home, he didn't want me spending time with her. Thankfully, I was able to stay true to my own heart here as well, and he was never able to sever us. It terrifies me to think about what would have happened if he had successfully destroyed my relationships with my mom and my sister. I'm not sure I ever would have broken away from him if he had. It also pains me greatly and gives me a tremendous amount of guilt to relive what I put them both through, what I put them all through. I have asked for, and received, their forgiveness. But when I think back to the insults, the anger, the way he treated the members of my family, I know that it will take more time and more healing before I can start to make any type of peace with this. I just take it one day at a time and trust in the healing process and the power of family and love. As survivors, we learn that we cannot change the past, only make peace with it as it comes hurling back at us. Our best defense is to accept that others have forgiven us, remember to forgive ourselves every time we are given an opportunity, and then look forward to tomorrow.

And my brother and his family? This was the toughest. I didn't see my brother again for a while after that brunch. He did put some distance between us, and rightfully so. Being so loving and protective of me, it was incredibly hard for my brother to witness the way I was treated by my husband. So, he avoided us as much as possible. My brother and his wife couldn't stand by and watch the torture, yet they couldn't ask me to leave him. How could they? It wasn't their place. They showed up as much as possible, and I will always be grateful to them for how much they did, but they could only take so much. They could only remain quiet for so long, and their limits were being put to the test every time we were all together. It was too much to ask and they needed frequent breaks, often long breaks, before they could come back and be near us again. When I finally made my escape, they were the first ones waiting for me at the hospital, and they have never left my side since. Blood is thicker than water? Our blood is thicker than concrete.

But what he put all of us through over the course of twenty years is hard to go back and revisit; yet somehow, I am often forced to do so when I see someone or something that brings back a memory. He would purposely embarrass me in front of them and know that they could not say anything. He would intentionally insult them and know that they would not say anything, nor would I. He would make us all as miserable as humanly possible in an effort to get my family to say, "enough is enough" and not come back to our home any longer. But I kept inviting and they kept coming because that is what family does when family is true and family loves. They witnessed more than they should have, they endured more than I could expect, but they kept showing up for me, and I will never forget that. He put an incredible strain on every single one of our relationships, but in the end, he couldn't make that final knockout punch, and that is something that we celebrate to this day. We are closer than ever, we survived, and my family is still everything to me. On this one, our trophy shelf is overflowing.

I shake my head and come back to the moment. I'm sitting in front of my laptop finishing off my blog for today. I choose my words carefully because, like the others, it's so difficult to write.

As much as we are victimized, tortured, hurt, scared, we still have decisions to make in life. At the time, it seemed that my only decision was to obey, to do what he told me to do. His words directed me, and the rest of reality was lost like leaves blowing in the wind. My reactions to his actions became my marching orders. I was robotic in response to his needs. Somewhere along the way I forgot I had a choice. I forgot that I could choose to reject what he said, or not do what he told me to do. But, as a victim of abuse, I also remember that facing the wrath caused by rebellion is not always worth it. It's scary, unpredictable, and typically a losing battle. It is just a horrible way to live when all of your choices are removed. It made me feel sad and hopeless.

You Are What You Do...

I have something that I would like to ask you to try on for me today. No, it's not a bathing suit (whew!) and it's not one of those annoying pairs of high heel shoes that look amazing on the shelf but when you put them on you can barely walk and your feet instantly hurt. Nope, it's easier, and harder, than that. Thank you in advance for doing this today because it could be something that is just the right fit for you.

Try on this concept: YOU ARE WHAT YOU DO. I heard this on television the other day and it made me think. In fact, I thought about it for days before I could even come close to writing about it and sharing it with you. I mean, really think about this. If we are what we do, then this really changes everything, doesn't it? That would mean that if we put the needs of our children first and protect them from harm, we are good mothers. That would mean that if we give to the needy, we are charitable. That would mean that if we were responsive to the needs of our friends, we are a good friend, right? It starts to make sense.

If we are dishonest then we are liars. If we yell at others, we are abusive. It starts to add up, doesn't it?

So, for all of those years that my then-husband called me awful names like fat, dumb, idiot, and ugly, what did that make me? Well, I took those insults and learned not to fight back so it made me a VICTIM. It certainly didn't make me fat, or dumb, or an idiot, or ugly. I was what I did, right? I stayed there and accepted that awful behavior from him, so I was, quite simply, his victim.

And for all of those years that he made all of the rules, kept me from my friends and family, controlled my every movement, evaluated my every step, and told me everything that I did was wrong, what did that make him? He was what he did right? It made him controlling, a bully, an abuser. This just keeps making more sense, doesn't it?

So, every day now, on the other side, I wake up and ask myself who I want to be. Because who I want to be is going to be a direct reflection of what I do in my life today. I want to be someone who helps others; therefore, I write a blog to advocate against domestic abuse. That makes me an advocate. I put my children first and try to protect them from harm, so that would make me a good mother. I am there when my friends need me, and even when they don't. I think they would agree that I am a good friend. I love my family and take every chance to tell them this and spend time with them. I hope I would be called a good family member. And I spend my days trying to help others, and so I hope that it would make me helpful and caring.

These are powerful words and a powerful idea that, in the end, our thoughts and our ideas mean something, too. That we can define our own selves as individuals through the choices we make and the actions we take rather than the ugly words that are thrown at us. If we truly are to be defined only by what we do in the world, only by what goodness we bring to the table, then by all means we can change the world right now by leaving a bad situation. Today could be the day that you go from victim to survivor simply by DOING. Are you ready? And so, this brings us back to where we began. If you are what you do and NOT what you are called, then who do you want to be today?

Remember this: STRENGTH + SUPPORT + PLAN = FREEDOM. You can do this.

It's a powerful concept I put out there today for all of us to try on for size. That we are defined by our own selves, not by how the world perceives us, but by who we are and what we do. The day I left and started fighting back I stopped being a victim and started seeing myself as a fighter. I started to see and believe that I was someone who could change her life by fighting back.

So many days his words rang through my head, "fat, dumb, lazy, idiot," and I had to challenge that each and every time and compare those words to what I had actually done in my life. Not even close! But for so many years I believed him. I believed him. Why? How? And why, even now, do I still hear those words on a really tough day? It happens to all of us, and our work is to remember that we define ourselves and to remember who we really are.

While still in our abuser's control, what do we hear in our heads on a dark night when we are trying to fall asleep and whose voice is it? What has he called us that we know deep in our hearts to be untrue? And even if some part of it were true, does he really have the right to call us that? Because who gave him the right to judge us? We did? Did we? How do we change that? We need to decide that is no longer ok. That today is the last day, tonight is the last night, and tomorrow is our new beginning. Then we reach out for help and start to make our plan. There's only one way out and it's in front of us, not behind us.

I publish this one with a sense of hope and a searing sadness at the same time. If I can inspire just one person, if you can hear me out there, if we can think differently today than we did yesterday, then I just did what I came here to do. And if I can remember to tell myself to think differently, too, to remember that I didn't deserve it, that I never was any of those things, I am victorious. I put my head down and silently pray. Please God, give me the strength to continue, to make a difference, to reach someone who needs me.

4

You May Now Kiss the Bride

> **WARNING SIGN OF DOMESTIC ABUSE:**
> Tells you that you are a bad parent or threatens to
> harm or take away your children

To tell my story is to have to straighten out and explain a lot. Not something new for the victim of domestic abuse and I'm sure you understand this. But for someone who is not a one in four, it can be challenging and confusing to read a story of a girl who walked into something horrific at age 21 and walked out at age 41. It is for this very reason that I walk slowly through the years to try and detail how things changed, how he changed, and how I tried to react and change alongside him to something that I never understood, was made to believe was my fault, and to somehow think I could fix. The most drastic of all of the years was when I was 25 years old because it was during this very time that he finally showed me who he was. That he didn't just have a temper with other people, but that he had no issue turning that temper on me. That he didn't have a cruel side just with others but that it was soon coming my way. And what changed the most during the year I turned 25? We got married.

I see her at age 25. Her wedding is something that she has dreamed about since she was a little girl, but as a little girl she had no idea what this year would actually be like when it got here. She is living in constant fear that her father will not be alive by the time her wedding day comes. A blinding, terrifying fear that keeps her awake at night, distracted during the day at work, and barely able to eat. She is fighting for a promotion at work that would set a company record; she would become the youngest executive ever appointed in her company, and it's taking all from her that she has left to give. After hours, they are building their first home. She is being asked to make choices about colors and bricks and counter-tops and faucets, an endless list of questions and decisions that she cannot escape. And she was planning every single detail of her wedding. A wedding she had dreamed of her entire life, but had stopped fantasizing about because it was not looking like the one that she had always seen in her mind when she was a carefree little girl and had believed that fairytales always came true.

She was so busy this year and so involved in so many things at once that she just showed up where and when he demanded that she show up, and if she wasn't with him, she was at work. As long as she met her deadlines for the house during construction and didn't disappoint him when he asked for something, he generally was less intense.

I see her on her wedding day. She is a blinding vision in white as she stands there and gives herself one final glance in the full-length mirror in her dressing room at the hotel. A glowing sequined gown and a veil that flows gracefully down her back like an ocean wave cascading into shore. Her hair and makeup done to perfection. Every detail accounted for. He comes to get her at her door and they head downstairs together.

Although she can feel the energy coursing through her veins, she had barely slept the night before and was glad for the adrenaline. It wasn't wedding jitters, for she didn't fear a thing about this day in front of her. It was pure anticipation of the day. The big day was finally here! She had lain in bed most of the night thinking about every detail of the next day: what she would look like, her family gathering around her, who was coming to the wedding. It was all really happening, and her father had made it. He had barely made it, but he had made it.

She was so young when they met, a mere twenty-one, and she had told him that she didn't want to rush into a relationship. He was more respectful of her back then; he didn't want to scare her away. She would go to her college classes all day, study, do her homework, and they would meet when he got home from work. He would take her to dinner, they would go to movies, and they would spend nights together. It was a perfect dream world and she never wanted to wake up. He took her to parties, he introduced her to all of his friends, and they even went on vacations together and laid on sunny beaches and went sightseeing around the US. They were a dream couple, a dream team, and she was happier than she had ever been in her life. She was living a fairy tale and had no idea yet how badly it would turn on her.

They dated for three years, then were engaged for another. She had four years to get to know this man who was now standing in front of her. They had lived together, they had traveled together, they had seen one another through sicknesses and stressful times, and they were so in love. He was the man of her dreams and perfect in every way. Did he want her all to himself? He did. But she loved the attention and was flattered by it. Did he want her to dress a certain way to please him? He did. But she didn't mind because she looked fine in whatever she put on. If he was happy, then she was happy and these little "asks" were so small. He was giving her a new life that she was ready to embrace to the fullest. She was about to walk down the aisle with him, and this was one of the happiest days of her life.

I see it now like you see one of those dreams that you are having where you want to see clearly what is going on but you are looking through a haze of white. You keep trying to focus on what is real and what is not, but all you see are blurry images blending together, while somewhere in your mind you are trying to tell yourself that this is not really happening, you're actually not sure if you are awake or dreaming.

I see them getting into the elevator together. She is so tiny in her dress and her train is flowing behind her making her look like a magical parade of one. I see them walking into the private room where all of their friends and family are waiting so they can take pictures together before the ceremony. Everyone tells her how beautiful she looks. Light is bouncing off of her in all directions. She is luminous and sparkling, and I see her through the haze.

She is surrounded by everyone in the world that she loves, and she silently thanks God for giving her this day. She closes her eyes for just a moment and thanks God again. It's been a close call and she knows that she has barely made it because he has barely made it. Her dad, her rock, the foundation of her life, had been diagnosed with cancer. She knew they would lose him any time now.

She had cried so many nights this past year as her heart slowly broke into a million little pieces. Nothing had been the same since the day he told her. He was her everything. The stress of planning the wedding coupled with the stress of knowing that she was going to lose her father was almost more than she could bear. Every day she would wake up, exercise, shower, go to work, and put on a brave face for the world. Inside she was slowly dying alongside her dad.

If he was going, she was going, too. This whole and beautiful and spirited girl would never be whole and beautiful again. He would one day soon leave this Earth, and with him he would take a piece of her. How much would be left behind she had no idea, but she knew that what would be left behind would be a broken and fragmented piece of her that may or may not resemble what was here before he left. She wasn't sure if she would ever heal. He was such a huge part of her. Life was swirling all around her while death was standing in the shadows, waiting for her father. She saw them there every day, life and death, like angry dance partners preparing to do a tango that would burn forever into her memory. A dance that she did not want to see. It was a year that she will never forget and yes, one that changed who she was forever.

She lost her dad to cancer a few months after her wedding. Therapists will tell her for years that she went from the safety of her father to what she thought was the safety of her husband.

Some will say that she was so heavily into the grieving process that she could not see what was coming. Others will say that something went wrong in her childhood and she never learned to stand up for herself.

I say that she was in love with a man she thought was her Prince Charming. He had worked for four years to cast a magical spell on her, and he had done a masterful job. He showed her so few warning signs of abuse. He showed so few red flags, and if he did, she was too young and too naïve to even see them. He was her knight in shining armor. He was her end-all-be-all. He was her man dressed all in white on their wedding day and off they went down the aisle looking like a perfect set of real life wedding cake toppers.

She had endowed him with larger-than-life qualities. Looking for Prince Charming was perhaps her first mistake – but she was too young, too naïve, to recognize the power she was vesting in him by expecting him to fill this roll, a role he readily accepted.

The changes started so soon it was actually frightening. I see them arriving at their suite for their honeymoon and he was immediately different. She had spent months planning their dream trip to Maui, and they had barely gotten into their room when he began criticizing her at an all-new level: the room was not "that great," this place looked "really boring" to him. "What are we going to do here for eight whole days?" he wondered out loud with a sour and disappointed tone to his voice.

What were they going to do in Maui for eight whole days? People spent their whole lives waiting for a vacation like this, and what were they going to do? She had spent months planning daily excursions of driving through mountains, snorkeling with sea turtles, exploring volcanoes, romantic honeymoon dinners right on the beach! What were they going to do? She showed him their plans, she showed him all her planning and how hard she had worked to put this together for them. She spread all the brochures along with their itinerary out on the bed and detailed their days for him. She bubbled over with enthusiasm as she delighted in what she had in store for them. "Eight days is a long time to be here, you should have made this four or five days," he sulked at her and then walked outside to see the view from the balcony.

And under the full bright moon of Maui, one of the most beautiful places on Earth, her heart began to feel its first large crack. She sat on the bed speechless, feeling disappointment drip down her body like a warm bucket of water had just been dumped on her head. *He would see, he would see that this was going to be amazing!* He was just tired, they had just gotten married, so that had to be it. They just needed a good night's sleep and they could start fresh in the morning. Little did she know what was coming her way or what was about to be taken away from her.

This blog is so important because it talks about another way that we can be abused - it addresses taking things away from us rather than hurling them at us. "I'll take the kids away from you," or "I'll keep the money away from you," or even, "I won't have sex with you unless or until..." They are always telling us what they will do, and these threats can become our reality.

Abuse comes in so many different forms, and if they can find a way to manipulate us, scare us, or torment us, even by removing things, they will. Taking from you, hurling at you, whatever hurts, hurts, whatever works, works.

You May Now Kiss the Bride

We kissed on the altar in front of all of our friends and family and it was the last time we ever kissed on the lips. EVER. For twenty years. I didn't know it that day, but it was a reality that I would live with for the rest of our marriage. We were already starting to break; I just didn't realize it. He was still charming; the insults were small. The control was minimal. I didn't know much about what was coming yet.

Domestic abuse can flow in two directions. It can come in giving and it can come in taking, so to speak. So often I talk about giving, about abuse that is sent towards us. The forward energy of abuse, like receiving insults flying at you all the time. The life we live with words of rage spewing towards our faces. We get too many directions, telling us what to do and when. Telling us what to say, what to wear, where to go, how to live. We get, get, get, get, get until we can't live with it anymore.

But there is the flip side of domestic abuse, one that I speak of less. That is the taking away that we suffer from, too. They take away affection. They take away our access to love, tenderness, and physical intimacy. They take away simple things like hugs and kisses that we, as human beings, so often crave. That can be just as painful as someone hurling insults at you when you love them. It is another way to break you down. It is the other side of domestic abuse. Another way to weaken and diminish both your spirit and your importance in their lives.

Abusers are gifted at knowing just what to do to make us feel fragile, sad, and isolated. They take away our access to money. They take away our access to friends and family. They may take away our personal freedom by checking our email, our voice messages, or our means of communicating with others, so we have no privacy left. They can take our cell phones, our car keys, anything that leads us to freedom. They know exactly what to do.

So, what else do they take? They take away our sense of who we are. The minute you get trapped inside of that soda can they start to change who you are. The once happy and shiny bubble that you were, full of life and vitality and energy, starts to cling to that wall inside the can. You face that "fight or flight" moment. If you decide to flee, and boy do I pray that you do at the very first sign of abuse, then you can most quickly get back to being that happy little bubble again. But the more you stay and cling, the weaker you get, and the weaker you get the harder it becomes to decide, up or down? Are you going to fight your way out to the top? Are you going to stay here forever in indecision? Or are you going to sink into the liquid and change into something that you were not when you began?

I sank into anxiety and depression as a result of clinging for so long, and in a very manipulative way he took away my access to getting help. He shamed me for having these issues, and it made me not want to seek help. For many years I tried to deal with this on my own. Domestic abuse + anxiety + depression? Wow, that's a lot to deal with alone. But it's so common, it's incredible. Who suffers from domestic abuse and is cheerful and steady on their feet? You are not alone here. In my case he said getting help and the medicines would cost too much. He accused me of being too weak to deal with it on my own. What did he do? He took away my ability to help myself. HE TOOK. He took to the point of my total incapacitation.

It doesn't really matter whether they give or take in a situation of domestic abuse. The bottom line is what is it doing to you? For twenty years he did not give me a birthday present. He told me he hated my birthday because I expected it "to be all about me that day." There's a giving and a taking that hurt, too. For twenty years he did not take me on a vacation that I selected because my needs were never important. There's a give and a take. It's really a word game, isn't it? Are they giving us pain or removing joy? Isn't it the same result anyway?

I think the scariest take of all is the threat that so many abusers put out to their wives and it is "I will take the children away from you and you will never see them again." My abuser left a note out in plain sight on the table in our den during our separation that said, "I will have 100% custody of the kids." I felt ice water run through my veins that day, and that was his intention. Well, I have news for you. Call the professionals and ask them what they think about that. This is where having a plan will mean the world to you.

I often say that life on the other side is not perfect and that there is work to be done. There is so much truth in that. You have to open your eyes very wide before you leave and plan for all scenarios so you see them all coming. That way, no matter what happens, you are ready and you know what you will be dealing with. When you are prepared and you have a plan you will feel safe and strong. When you feel safe and strong you will be ready. When you are ready then there is nothing that anyone can give you or take away from you that you will be worried about. You just need to know how to do this the right way by putting safety first. So, what do I say to that? I say GIVE yourself a plan and don't let anyone TAKE it away.

Remember this: STRENGTH + SUPPORT + PLAN = FREEDOM. You can do this.

_____

I look back on those days with so much sorrow and sadness. How cruel of a world where a young girl thinks she has met the man of her dreams only to find out, within twenty-four hours of marrying him, that he is not who she thought he was. Here I was over 4,000 miles from home in Hawaii on my honeymoon, watching my new groom turn into someone that I could not recognize. It was a long and painful eight days. It was a horrible honeymoon because he didn't want it to be a good one. All of that self-control and discipline that he had exercised to make me fall in love with him was no longer needed, and as he dropped the mask I found myself on my honeymoon with a total stranger. I was scared, I was stunned, and I remember feeling sad and subdued when I saw the other couples laughing and acting silly. They were celebrating and I was thinking, "Why aren't we? Why aren't we doing funny hula dances and holding hands and taking moonlit strolls here in Maui?" And the answer was because he didn't want to. He wanted to get through these eight days with me and get home and get started with our life together as husband and wife. I was his now. He had a ring on my finger to prove it. No more Mr. Nice Guy. No more acting required. Our real life together was just beginning.

It continued like this when we got home, this new him that I did not know and me still the same person. This horrible mismatch of people who did not belong together, who had just walked down the aisle, made promises "till death do us part," were somehow expected to make something work that felt like a terrible mistake. I was a loving and affectionate young girl who craved hugs and kisses and was pushed away and silently rebuffed when she came to him for love or attention. A young girl who begged to cling to the man of her dreams while she watched her father die of cancer only to hear, "I'm not really a hugging type person." The shock, the horror, the sadness, the despair. How could I not experience anxiety or depression? How could any of us not?

I would sit next to him on the sofa, he would place a pillow between us so that we would not accidentally touch one another. I wanted to climb in his lap and hide, I wanted to crawl into his arms and feel safe, I wanted him to kiss me and show me that he loved me, I wanted him to tell me that he loved me. I wanted. And I never received. Because he took away. He broke my heart so badly I didn't think there was a way it would ever come back together. Not all the stitches, nor all the glue, nor all the kings' horses nor all the kings' men. Who could put this smashed heart back together? The pain was so raw, so unbearable, so shocking, and so unexpected. He simply closed the door on the man he had been, and I never saw that man again. What the hell had just happened here? This was at a time when the pain was still so new and so raw that I felt every bit of it. It was like feeding your heart through a paper shredder one inch at a time. I felt every single knife cut, and I was bleeding out emotionally. I didn't know what was happening and I didn't know why it was happening and I didn't know how to stop it. Who do we turn to when this happens? How do we explain that we have just come home from our honeymoon and we don't want to be here? How could we possibly deal with the embarrassment and failure of that?

So, I stayed. Why did I stay? Because I was about to lose the foundation of my life, my father, to cancer at any moment? Perhaps. Because I had just gotten married and was exhausted and thought my mind was playing tricks on me or that maybe I was overreacting? Maybe. Because I believed in love and thought I could quickly recover the man with whom I just spent the last four years? Of course. I could do that, in a flash, in a snap, in a spark of love. Because I still believed in sparks in love.

———————

I see her at age 41, she is getting ready to leave him. He places that chilling note out in their den for her to read: "I will have 100% custody of the kids." He places it right in the room where he has held her captive on so many hopeless nights. He places it in the room where he has trapped her with the fury of his words and the threats in his voice. He places it in the room where she felt the most imprisoned in her home because it was his favorite room and once she wandered in he rarely let her leave without punishing her for several hours on end.

And now she wanders in one day when he is not home to see that note with those horrifying words and the largest threat he has ever made. He has a plan to take their children away from her. She has never felt more fear in her life. She has never felt more terror. He has raged at her for twenty years, he has followed her when she has tried to get away, he has warned her not to leave him, but today, more than any other day, she feels the fear of what leaving him could do to her.

In the midst of her terror, she is rational; there is a reservoir of strength deep inside she calls on to protect her children. That rational self takes out her cell phone and snaps a photo of the note without touching it. She wants to act as if she never saw it and not give him any more power than he was looking for, but the terror remains. She walks quietly up the stairs to her room, walks into her closet, closes the door and locks it. Then she calls her lawyer and tells her what she has just seen. Her lawyer bursts out laughing,

"That will never happen Susan," she says. "He's just trying to scare you. Not in a million years." And her lawyer was right. It didn't happen, and wouldn't have in a million years. But it's an abuser's tool to threaten and scare us, and it worked that day until she had the sense to snap out of it and do a reality check with a professional. It was the first time she consciously realized that what he said was not her reality. It was a very powerful moment. She was so grateful that it occurred to her to make that call.

———

I wrote this blog with a sense of power and strength coursing through my body even though it reads as so particularly sad. He took and he took for over twenty years, yet I sit here today and I take back. I take back my power, I take back my purpose, and I take back my willingness to live, to love, and to share my heart, vulnerability, and feelings with the world again. The journey was so painful it took me to the brink. I saw and experienced things that I didn't want to see and will never be able to erase from my mind. But I sit here now, in front of my laptop, with the power and ability to change a life simply by saying this: you don't have to let them take anything else from you anymore. How much is too much? How long is too long? How much do you have left to give away anyway?

5

It's YOU Not Me

I remember something he used to say to me all the time, "This is your job, not mine." I don't think in twenty years he ever used the word "our." He never said, "This is our problem to figure out," or "This is our job to raise this family, so what do you think we should do?" "We" is another one that I never heard, because in the world of domestic abuse they are never on your team. It is always you vs. them, and them vs. the world. It's very clear once you see it and live it.

When I left my corporate job in order to have children everything became "my job," and nothing became his job. I had made enough money to set us up for a very bright future, and so he had stopped working altogether. We had enough money to have housekeepers, nannies, gardeners, cars with drivers, but he would have none of that. He didn't want strangers in our home, he didn't want people walking around outside on our lawn, and he didn't want me to spend our money that way; he fought me endlessly when I mentioned that I could use some help, and I ended up doing everything myself.

Then, everything became "your job," as in, "It's your job Susan to take care of everything inside of this house and that means the children, the laundry, the cooking, the grocery shopping, the cleaning, the dog, the bills and finances, (although he kept the reins tight over the money and only moved funds over once I showed what we owed on our bills), and everything that happens in here. You don't work, so this is your job. And I'll take care of the lawn and the pool. That will be my job." He divided up the work in this horribly uneven way, and off he went. I lived the life of three full time workers, and he lived the life of a pool boy.

I see her at age 33. She is coming in from the grocery store with the baby in one arm and about five grocery bags slung on her other arm. She throws her purse down on the counter before her arm gives out and she puts the baby in his swing. She dashes back out to the garage to bring in the rest of the groceries knowing better than to ask him for help. Grocery shopping is "her job," so he will not help bring the groceries in from the car. When she comes back in the room he was standing there with an evil grin on his face. "Where's your purse he asks?" "It's right there," and she points to where it had been. Only her purse is missing and in its place where it had been sitting on the kitchen counter is a pair of filthy and disgusting work boots covered in wet and dripping mud. "What did you do!" she exclaims at him, "Why did you put your work boots on the counter where my purse was?"

"Do you have any idea how filthy your purse is?" he sneers at her, "It's the same as putting those disgusting boots on the counter. Now clean that up and don't ever do that again. And if I ever catch you putting your purse there again you will find my work boots right back there, covered in mud or maybe worse."

He missed the part where she came dashing in with their thirty-pound baby on one arm, grocery bags on the other. He missed the part where she was bringing in the groceries by herself because he wouldn't help. And he missed the part where she was showered and dressed and at home from the grocery store early enough in the day to have time to clean their home and get their dinner on the table once she put everything away. All he saw was her purse on the counter, and that was enough for him to move into attack mode because she had done something wrong again.

Is it like this for you? This is what every single day was like for her. No matter what she did, no matter how hard she tried, no matter how pretty, no matter how sweet, no matter how smart, no matter how hard she worked, no matter how much she tried to be different than the day before when he hated everything she had done, she would do something new the next day that would set him off again. She began to hate coming home.

She cleans up the mud, puts his work boots away, puts away the groceries, put their baby down for his nap, and begins cooking dinner. A dinner that would be criticized because he hated her cooking and thought his was far superior.

I see her during her thirties, and it's like watching a trailer for a bad horror movie. I see her glowing and pregnant with their first child at the age of thirty-one: he is looking at her one day in her new maternity outfit and calling her huge and fat. She runs to the bedroom and cries. He later tells her that everyone else he knows was able to stay thin during their pregnancy, why couldn't she? I remember that morning, pulling that beautiful outfit out of the bag and putting it on. It looked pretty good. Yes, I was getting bigger, I was pregnant! But it was cute and I was still early into the pregnancy, first trimester, and I thought I looked fashionable and fun. He took one look at me and said, "Wow, look at how fat you are."

I felt the sting of his words, I felt the sting of humiliation and worst of all, I felt a huge surge of helplessness in knowing there was nothing I could do about it. I couldn't get smaller and I couldn't diet. I was pregnant! I was stuck. Now what was I going to do for the next six months? I hated him with every fiber of my being. I hated him for making me feel bad about myself. I hated him for not telling me that I was beautiful no matter what during my pregnancy. I hated him for never supporting me or being proud of me or being grateful that my body was making a human life for us. What the hell was the matter with him? I simply hated him in that moment, and hate is a horrible emotion to feel when you are growing a human miracle inside of your body.

I see her at the end of the pregnancy, belly large with life and barely able to move without huffing and puffing. He has bought a new set of patio furniture for around the pool and put it all in the basement still inside the large brown cartons. There is a picture on the outside of each box showing what is inside and what it will look like once assembled. He calls her down to show it to her and she comes down and says that it looks lovely. "Great," he says with a smile, "Then you can put it all together before your family comes over tonight so we can use it." "What?" she asks hoping he is joking but already knowing that he is not. "Yes," he says with a look that she already knows will not waiver, "I got this for your family so we can all sit around the pool. You can't go in the pool since you are nine months pregnant so you need to put this all together. I'll go get my tools." She sinks to her knees knowing there is no reason to try and fight her way out of this, she is going to spend her day putting together a new patio furniture set made for eight people. As she takes the pieces out of the first box she tries to lean in and start putting the pieces together but her large belly is in the way and she cannot reach. "Look," she tells him, "This is going to be impossible. I can't reach anything." "Oh! Wait!" and he disappears and then comes back and hands her a long plain looking metal rod, "What is this?" she asks confused. "This is a drill-bit extender," he explains, "Now you can put it on the drill and the drill will reach all of the furniture with your big stomach in the way. See? Problem solved. Make sure you tighten everything well so it doesn't break when you sit on it." And off he went.

I see her nursing their sweet baby in the middle of the night, a whopping baby boy! This baby could not get enough to eat, day or night. She turns the light on to better she what she is doing and he angrily rolls over and demands that she turn off the light because she is disrupting his sleep. She sits there stunned at what she has just heard and he angrily repeats himself thinking she did not hear him. She clumsily obeys, so tired, so sleep-deprived, and walks with their precious baby into the nursery to finish feeding him. He tells her not to ever turn that light on again in the middle of the night, he needs his sleep. For months she will reel over this. He needs his sleep? She is nourishing their baby through her breast to give him life and the best possible nutrition. She knows that other husbands will wake up in the middle of the night just to sit with their wives while they breastfeed, and she knows that other husbands will take "bottle duty" in the middle of the night while they supplement their baby so the mom can get a true night's sleep. But she gets one thing and one thing only: she gets a complaint to stop disrupting his sleep. She reels from the harshness of her world, she hurts from the raw pain that she is handed daily, and she steels herself as she knows now that she is fighting for two. She can't break now because she has created a human life that will need her and depend on her for the next two decades at least. She has no choice but to turn off that light and go to another room and not engage in battle with an enemy so forceful that he can knock her over with words, scare her with threats, and make her so sad in the middle of the night that she stumbles blindly into the room next door to continue to breastfeed their firstborn baby boy.

I see them going to the hospital to have their second child, she is thirty-four now, another whopping baby boy! Except he is so big that she will labor all night long. A very long and deliberate and painful labor for her. They cannot give her enough drugs to keep her comfortable. She is in agony. He is in a sour mood and complaining all the while because he has a sore throat. He is not focusing on her or her labor in any way; making no pretenses this time, he simply does not seem to care. He pages the nurse and she finally feels a surge of relief. Maybe he does notice her agony and is going to see what can be done to make her more comfortable? But as the nurse walks in she cannot believe her ears. He asks the nurse for some Tylenol to help with his sore throat. Then he asks her to turn off the light so he can go to sleep. He complains about his small bed in the delivery room and how he wishes he was at home. She labors all night, alone in the dark, feeling like the only person left on the planet.

She sits alone in the darkness that night and marvels at what is going on. She is pregnant with their second baby. She is supposed to be the center of the universe right now, or at least the center of attention in this hospital room! But he and his sore throat and his need to sleep have taken center stage. She lays there in agony for hour after hour, contraction after contraction, and has no one to tell how bad it hurts, no one to wipe the sweat off her forehead as it runs down her face and stings her eyes, no one to keep her company in anticipation of this new child. She has no one. She looks around the room and the realization hits her with force. The thought is so painful to her and so sad that she wants to cry. But she doesn't want him to wake up and hear her. She doesn't want to be mocked or chastised for crying, so she lays there silently in the worst pain of her life and labors with their second child until she sees the sun start to stream through the curtains in their room the next morning.

She sees the doctor come in to check on her and ask her "how they did" overnight and she wants to spit at him and start screaming. "How did we do? We?? We did nothing! We did horrible, we suck!" But she sits there silently as if it is a rhetorical question while he checks her vital signs and she quietly asks for more pain medication as she has done every time someone has walked in for the past fourteen hours. "Wow!" he says looking at the paper readout that is chugging out alongside her bed, "Looks like you had some really big contractions overnight. How did you handle that?" She looks down and tries not to burst into tears. She lays back and puts her head on the pillow and closes her eyes. How did she handle that? She handled it alone in the dark trying not to scream while her husband slept like a peaceful lamb with his little sore throat, that's how she handled that. She feels betrayed and furious. How did they not know that she was dealing with these huge contractions? How did someone not notice that her husband had gone to sleep and left her for dead? Why didn't anyone ever step up to help her, and why couldn't she just say what she was thinking, "Does anyone in here realize that I'm having a baby and have basically been abandoned by all of you at once? Does someone want to get off of your ass and help me please? Because I feel like my body is about to rip into two pieces." But to complain will come back at her, to be vocal is never helpful, so she simply and quietly asks, "Could I have some more pain medication please?" and the doctor pages the nurse to get her some, "stat."

Her heart is breaking now in ways that she knows cannot be mended. But at thirty-four, with a new baby and a beautiful toddler, it is not the time to deal with it. So, she pushes the pain down to a far deeper place to deal with at another time. And she knows that this is not the end. It is the beginning of something that will take on a life of its own and become so large and so unstoppable that one day it will walk up to her and confront her and she will have no choice other than to look it in the eye and give it an answer as to what the hell she has been doing all of this time.

I see flashes of her during those years. The baby is crying, "Why can't you get him to stop?" he would demand. Dinner is late, "Why can't you get anything done on time?" he would growl. She stumbles to the table in a state of disrepair, "Another day without a shower? Really?" he would look at her like she was a piece of garbage. And she felt like one. She felt like a dirty piece of trash that should just be thrown into the trash bin and done away with already. "Why can't you be like the other mothers?" he would ask her. "They manage to cook and clean and take a shower. I see them all the time. They look great to me."

But the other mothers she knew were struggling the same way that she was. She wasn't sure what "other mothers" he was even referring to. The "other mothers" that really had their acts together had help at home. They had nannies and housekeepers and cooks who lived with them, and so they had the time to take a shower or buy a new outfit; they had the time and resources to tend to how they looked. But he had forbidden her to get help. "Why do you need help? Everyone else can do this, why can't you?" And so, she did it all on her own, without a shower, serving him dinner late, giving everything she had to her two precious babies before anyone else, and somehow, like all the "other mothers" that she knew, she made it work.

I see her as the years go by and the boys slowly grow and thrive and gain more independence each passing year. They are her beacons of hope. They are her pride and joy. They are, quite simply, what keeps her going and getting up and moving every single day. They fill her heart with a love and a joy that she never even knew to be possible. And so, when many ask her why she stayed so long, well, she was busy raising her sons, and that is all that she needed to worry about at the time.

And I see her on that one ominous day, she is now thirty-nine years old, driving her large white SUV through the streets of their town as the sky grows dark and black and looks like it is closing down on her. Her cell phone rings and he yells out, "Where are you!"

"I'm on the main road by the school," she answers. "Go get the boys!" he screams, "Get the boys and bring them home! There is a tornado warning and I don't want them in that old building. Go get them and bring them home right now!"

"Ok!" she answers as she makes a U-turn and pulls into the school parking lot. She had no idea there was a tornado warning, but the sky is turning black right before her eyes and she is terrified.

She runs into the school building and personnel are moving quickly in every direction. "We are about to go into lockdown!" the school secretary tells her. "If you want your boys pull them right now or they will be here for a long time!" "Pull them!" she says and runs into the hallway with fear and adrenaline coursing through her entire body.

Moments later she sees her boys come rushing down the hallway with their book bags and looks of fear and confusion on their faces.

"What's going on mom?" they both ask. "A storm," she says calmly and smiles. "We just need to go to the car and drive home and we're fine." "Where is dad?" they both ask in fear.

"He's waiting for us at home," she answers. "We'll all go down to the basement just in case." She is smiling and calm the whole time but her heart is racing and she is terrified. Is this really the best idea? Should she be out on the road? It's too late to turn back, so she takes the boys and they rush to the car.

The sky opens up like a faucet on full stream and she can barely see the road as she is driving. The five-minute drive home feels like an hour. The boys are completely quiet as they watch the sky get darker and then her son announces "Mom! The sky is turning green!" right as they turn into their neighborhood. She is trying not to panic, she knows they are one minute from home, she doesn't see any cloud formations, and she is driving as fast as she can while looking out for other cars, animals, anything that could be out on the street.

She sees their home in front of them and tears of relief fill her eyes. She pushes the button to open the garage door and it seems to take forever to open. "Hurry!" her youngest yells, "Mom! Lightning!" and the bang of thunder and flash of light is so bright that it seems as if it is striking right next to them. She rushes to pull into the garage and in a moment of fear and misjudgment she bangs her side mirror on the garage wall as they pull in. Not having time to worry about it, she closes the door, rushes the boys inside and they all run into the basement where he is waiting.

"I did it!" she calls out. "We're here!"

"Mom hit the garage!" her son announces with the excitement that only a little boy could muster in a moment like that. He had breaking news and he was excited to share it. She is panting with residual fear and exhaustion as she comes down the final stairs into the basement, and she stops dead in her tracks as she sees his expression change. The storm clouds that were outside were nothing compared to the storm clouds that she sees darken his face.

He slowly moves toward her in a way that she will never forget. Chills run down her spine as she stands motionless, trapped by her own fear, not knowing what is going to happen next. She wants to back away. She knows this feeling all too well. This feeling that she must run, hide, get away; but she knows that there is nowhere to go. Wherever she goes he will follow. Wherever she hides he will seek. It is a hopeless and helpless scenario that she has lived with for so many years that she just simply stands still and feels sick to her stomach. His eyes look like laser beams of white hot hatred and she, in turn, experiences pure white terror as the words shoot out directly at her, one inch from her face. "YOU DID WHAT?" She shrinks back in fear unable to say a single word.

This is the life of the victim of domestic abuse. For, no matter what we do that is right, we are always called out for what we do that is wrong. Did it matter that I did a U-turn that day, raced into a chaotic school, got my boys out and brought them home in time to avoid a tornado that was heading towards our town? Of course not. What was always mentioned about that day was this: the day you hit the garage on the way home from the storm.

From the vantage point of the average person, this encounter may seem mundane. Yes, he was nasty. No, he did not acknowledge the fear and danger they had faced getting home. No, he was not grateful they were safe. But he did not threaten, right? There was no physical abuse, right?

Unless you have faced emotional abuse, you can neither understand nor appreciate the terror it evokes. Implicit is the need to degrade and denigrate; implicit is the accusation that you are less than, that you never fail to disappoint, that you can do nothing right; and implicit is the threat that it will eventually – and the victim never knows when that will be – take him past the point of his usual anger and "now you've done it," he will turn violent.

The words flow for this blog, so easy to write, I could write an entire book about being wrong. I was wrong for twenty years. We are all wrong, victims of domestic abuse, we are always wrong. Even when we are right they will twist every last detail until they prove that we are wrong.

It's YOU Not Me...

There is a breakup line that has become so common that it is now cliché: "It's not you. It's me." We see this all the time in movies and TV shows. The man takes the woman out to dinner, a public place where she will not make a scene, to break up with her. She sits there devastated and asks what she did wrong and he says, "It's not you. It's me." It's the perfect way to take the blame, get out scot-free, get away, and do the very best not to upset her.

In the world of domestic abuse, we have to turn everything upside down to see reality. Our world is backwards from everyone else and we do not have a normal. Their husbands take out the trash. We are yelled at for hours if our trashcans become too full. Their husbands buy toilet paper at the supermarket. We are yelled at for using too much toilet paper in one week.

When you begin to understand that you may be living a life of domestic abuse, or you have already discovered this fact, then you are already heading in the direction of understanding that you cannot go to someone with a typical relationship or a typical life to ask them for help or advice. They do not understand your world. This is not to suggest that you shut out your support network of friends and family; by all means, they are your world! But seek out the professionals who will understand what your real world is like so that they can get you out of that world safely because they truly know, understand, and are trained to help you.

For many years I sought neither advice nor support from anyone because I recognized that my world was so different from everyone else's and didn't think that anyone would or could understand. That is the sting and the humiliation of domestic abuse. So, I kept mine hidden and attempted to live with it. I didn't think "thehotline.org" was meant for someone like me. I thought it was meant for those other women who were being hit and thrown down by their husbands. I didn't understand that being trapped in a room and not being allowed to leave, or being told what to do at every moment was also a reason to call. I didn't understand that if every single thing I did was wrong and I was made to pay for it, that I was different enough to call. Don't judge for yourself. Don't judge at all. They won't. If you call, they will help. They will understand.

Last year I was shopping in a store and I saw this shirt and I stopped in my tracks to look at it. It said, "It's YOU not ME." I stood there stunned and thought, "That is my life! Someone finally understands me!" It was him not me. It was always him. That is not to say that I was perfect. No one is. That is not to say that I did everything right because no one does. But in a world of domestic abuse, when you are the victim, everything that you do wrong and everything that makes you less than perfect no longer matters because the truth of the matter is that all the bad behavior belongs to your partner. His behavior is so much bigger than the flaws and mistakes that you bring to the table that you actually cannot take the blame because you are living in a world that is upside down. It's them, NOT YOU.

I bought that shirt on the spot, and I've worn it so many times that you can barely make out what it says anymore! I wear it on good days, I wear it on bad days, I wear it to feel powerful, I wear it to make me laugh, and most of all I wear it to remember something that every SODA™ should be wearing on our shirts every single day. We did nothing wrong. We were abused. It's all them and we deserve better than that.

What have you done wrong today? I mean really. What have you done wrong today?

Remember this: STRENGTH + SUPPORT + PLAN = FREEDOM. You can do this.

On a day like today I stop to remember all of the things that I did right. I graduated college with honors. I had once been a nicely paid model in my home town. I earned that darn promotion and became the youngest Director ever appointed in my company at the age of twenty-five. I was a technology wizard. I was a pretty good writer who still could figure out how to string a few words together. I was a dedicated mom. I was a volunteer in my community who gave endless hours to helping others, even when I could barely help myself. I had a list of things that I did right that was noteworthy.

Yet, here I was living a daily life hearing about how everything I did was wrong. When did that happen? How did that happen? Why did that happen? That's the funny thing about abuse – it doesn't just happen. We don't wake up one day and get insulted and think, "That's it I'm outta here." It happens slowly over time, and we don't see it happening at first. Then it happens more. Then it happens even more. And all the while we are building a life together, a home together, a family together, and looking at a future together, and one day you realize that you are in a place that you do not want to be. And you have a scary and painful decision to make. Do I stay and live with this, or do I have the right to make a better life for myself? And you are asking yourself this while reverberating from all the put-downs, all the insecurity he has inflicted on you. How much does it take until you break?

I publish this blog with a feeling of pure red-hot anger. I did so many things right during our life together. I cooked. I cleaned. I made a lovely home. I gave birth to two of the most beautiful boys on this planet. And I raised them with so much love (and still do)! But none of that would matter to him because I could not continue to be the Stepford Wife that he so wanted and the rest of the world thought I was. I would be shamed every day for being less than perfect, for being human, for trying my best, a best that was never good enough. Yes, I can feel the pure red-hot anger course through my veins. I never deserved that. You don't deserve that. No one deserves that.

I approached every day with an open heart, a heart that bore endless scars from his abuse. I kept a smile on my face for all to see, tried to be the wife he wanted me to be, tried my best to love him even when he tried his best not to let me, and attempted to survive in a world where there are no winners and rarely any survivors to celebrate. So, in the end what did I really do right? I finally left.

6

Slow and Steady Wins the Race

I can still see it as if it is sitting right in front of me. It was a single piece of paper with two columns on it and at the top he had written "Monthly Budget." One night after we had both stopped working he yelled at me for hours about how much I had spent that month when he saw our bills come in. The next day he came into the room and said, "Sit down, we are going to talk." It wasn't a question, it was a command. I had just put both of the boys down for a nap and it was a motherhood miracle to get these two to sleep at the same time, so I was looking forward to an hour or so of time just for me. But he had waited for this moment, too, and he pounced on me the second he saw me alone.

"We're going to make a list," he said with a very serious look on his face.

"A list of what?" I ask as I slowly sit down with the usual fear and anxiety building within me.

"We are going to make a list of every single thing that you think you need to buy every month and for what reason. Then I am going to approve it. Then we are going to make it into your monthly budget." I sit there feeling stunned and not able to react. "Let's go," he says, "How much do you need to spend at the drugstore and what do you need?"

"Are you serious?" I ask feeling fear and nervousness build inside of me, "I don't know what I need every month at the drugstore, how could I possibly know?"

"Well," he says, "We need to start somewhere so you are going to take a guess, we are going to make a list of everything you think you need every month, and I don't care how long this takes, we are going to do the drugstore, the grocery store, your doctors, your food, your gifts for the children, your gifts for the family, your hairspray, your toothpaste, every single thing you buy every single month until we are done."

"Please tell me you are joking," I say as I look into his eyes.

"Why would this be funny?" he asks me with a dead serious look on his face, "If I leave you alone with the money you will spend all of it, so someone has to watch what you're doing. Now, how many times a year do you need to buy a new tube of toothpaste?"

This list takes days to finish. It was one of the worst and most painful and tedious projects he ever made me work on with him, but he wouldn't relent. And when it was done it became a single piece of paper with two columns on it listing exactly how much money I was allowed to spend every month. If I went under I was fine, but if I went over, boy was there going to be a problem. And it wasn't like I could just say, "My hair cut costs $75.00," it was more like I would have to explain how much my hair cut costs, why I went to that salon, why I couldn't go to the cheaper place in the mall where I took our children and why I couldn't find a place to cut my hair for $15.00. It went for days on end until he produced that nasty piece of paper that I wanted to use as kindling in our fireplace. But instead it sat square on the desk in my home office and stared me down every time I walked in there because I knew if I didn't look at it I would be looking at it with him at the end of the month.

It bears repeating that I had made enough money for neither of us to have to work again for the rest of our lives. And it bears repeating that he quit his job never to work again. I stopped working to have children, but I always knew that I would work again because I love to make a difference in the world and feel in my heart that there will always be a place for me to do so. So, for him to put me to this extreme was difficult to deal with. Because if I went over by a penny, one single penny, we would be talking about it at the end of the month. Would I have minded living on a budget? No. I live on a budget now, and I am very happy to do so. However, he put me on a budget that was nearly impossible to live on, when we had more than enough money to live on double the amount, and he set me up for a monthly failure that would come at me like a wrecking ball to the side of my head. The bills would come, he would go to get the mail, and my hands would start to shake. He became a trigger for something new to me: panic attacks.

I didn't fully understand what was going on or why, but I knew that when he was around and I could not get away I started to feel an overwhelming sense of fear. When I could predict that his anger was coming my way, I would experience a dizzying feeling. I would start to see spots out of the corners of my eyes, I would feel my face get hot, and I would start to sweat at my temples. If I could get away from him, I could sometimes calm myself. But if I could not, each symptom would get worse until sweat was pouring down my face and I looked and felt like I had just finished a marathon. Not only was it scary and a really shaky feeling from head-to-toe, but I would feel exhausted for hours afterward as my body would recover from whatever it was that I had just gone through. He became the trigger to my worst nightmare come true. You could now actually see my fear. I was running out of places to hide from him and from the world.

I see her the year she turns 40. A year where time stood still and everything changed in a way that there was no going back. I see her falling down the stairs and crushing her right arm, him hovering over her, her screaming out in terror. I see her unable to move, stranded in bed, him not speaking to her. I see her fear as she feels it. I see her panic as he comes near her. I see the pain she is in and how she is begging for her prescription pain pills, but he will not get them. I see her mother leave the house and go get them for her. I see her mother not wanting to leave her there with him so she waits for him to leave to run his own errands, and her mother coming back as quickly as possible. I see the relief in both of their eyes as she gets her medicine and her mother is back at her side, watching over her, making sure she is safe.

I see what is left of her youth. I see her pale and white and fragile. So fragile that a large wisp of wind could break not only her bones but what is left of her spirit. I see what she has been through for almost twenty years. I see that she has tried to survive, tried to love, and tried to understand. I see that she has no more answers today than she did at 21. I want to sit down and cry for her. I want to sit down and cry with her. I want to sit down and cry. I see what the years with him have done to her. I see her.

I see the last months they had together before her fall. They were frantic and scary months and for the first time she is beginning to realize that this will never change and he will never change. He is getting nastier with each passing day, having less patience with her, hiding less of his anger and disdain, and she is feeling more terrified than she ever has. She hides from him as much as possible during the day, coming out only in the afternoons to take care of the boys and retreating to the bedroom at night as soon as she puts the boys to bed.

I see him yelling at her all the time now, about anything and everything. I see that everything she does seems to make him furious. I see that if there was ever any love, it has now turned to pure hatred and that is like handing an even bigger weapon to an abuser. He sees that she is trying to retreat from him as often as possible, and he senses that he is beginning to lose her. This makes him angrier, more desperate, and so he chases her down more often. It becomes a vicious cycle of cat and mouse, tiger and prey.

Consciously or subconsciously, she is beginning to recognize that the end is near. In a frightened and final attempt not to lose herself forever, she starts to build a life for herself outside of their home. It's not so much of a conscious plan as it is a gut instinct that she needs to stay connected to the outside world and reconnect with as many people as possible as he moves in closer and closer for what feels like the kill. She somehow feels that if she surrounds herself with people, he will have a harder time reaching her; if more people are focused on her whereabouts and daily activities, he might back off. Each day her panic attacks grow, her fear for her future grows, and her survival instinct screams louder and louder that she must get out before it is too late. She is finding herself and losing herself simultaneously. She is finding a person that she hasn't seen in a while, a person who knows how to make things happen and get things done in the world, the person she last saw in the workplace. And she is losing herself more and more as simple things like going to the grocery store, driving too far from home, and being alone with her husband now terrify her in ways that have never been that scary before.

In an act of bravery and total defiance, she has taken a volunteer position at the elementary school's PTA. This places her at the center of her community where she becomes very visible. Whatever the school does, she is involved. Whatever events the school holds, she is there. It is the perfect place for her to be. Not only is she giving back to those who need her, but she is surrounded by a careful and watchful community of loving families and school personnel who do not know that she is in danger but will surely notice if something happens to her. She begins to feel a new sense of security that she hasn't felt since she entered the spider's web two decades before. And as he sees himself losing control of her, his fury rises.

Her life has now hit a crescendo at home, so scary that she is afraid to go to bed at night. He is not speaking to her, and the doctor has ordered that she continue to recover alone in bed from the fall down the stairs so as not to be bumped, so she is the only one sleeping in her bed. She locks the door at night and jams a chair under the doorknob for fear that he will kill her in her sleep. He yells and threatens her now all the time when they are home alone together, but he will not speak to her and have a normal conversation. He traps her in rooms. When she tries to leave he follows her wherever she goes and will not stop until she breaks and agrees with whatever he is yelling about, gives in, tells him what he wants to hear, and agrees to what he wants her to say. She is so exhausted she will do whatever it takes to make him stop attacking her. She just wants him to leave her alone. She prays every night that he will just leave her alone.

This is when the dreams begin. She falls asleep every night trying to block out what has happened that day that has greatly upset her as she feels the pain and fear wash over her one final time when she closes her eyes. She tries not to think about how bad things have gotten and what he has done to her that day, as her mind tries to make her watch a movie that she does not want to see. She just wants to sleep and pretend that she is ok, that life is ok, that none of this is really happening. Going to bed has become the best and worst part of the day, her escape and her prison all at once. When she truly sleeps she can escape the horror of her life; but when she dreams she relives the events of her days all over again, only to wake and find out that the nightmare was not a nightmare at all. The nightmare is her life.

During this time, she starts having the repetitive dreams where she finally gets the courage to tell him that she wants a divorce. In her dream each night they are in a different place and she chooses different words; but in her dream each night she accomplishes her goal. She tells him that she wants a divorce and he agrees without an argument. She feels a sense of peace and calm wash over her body like she has never felt before right as she is waking up. She feels light as a feather and happier than she has in years. She can feel the cleansing in her sleep, and she is so overtaken that she does not realize that she is dreaming. Then, slowly, each morning as her eyes open, her left thumb immediately reaches over to her left ring finger to feel for it. The second she feels the band – something she now views as a handcuff – she knows it was a dream and her eyes fill with tears and her heart with despair. Her stupid wedding ring! It is still there, on her ring finger. It was another dream. She would open her eyes, see that she was still in her bedroom and feel a blackness wash over her like a cancer running a sprint through her veins. Her alarm clock would sound, she would know her boys were waiting for her, and she would get out of bed and start another day.

Those awful nightmares. I can't tell you how long this went on, but it must have been at least the last year of my marriage, taking me right through to the age of 41. The beauty of dreaming that I was free, to wake up to the horror that I was still imprisoned. Imprisoned within my own large, sprawling mansion that I had bought for us. I had bought my own prison. Made of ivory bricks and lovely windows. Spiral staircases and marble floors. The nicest prison you've ever seen. I bought it myself. With the money I made. From my corporate success. And here I was, trapped.

How does that happen? How can someone become so successful, earn so much money, and still get trapped in their own life? We already know that it's easier than you might think. He took control of our money the moment I started making it. He put me on a spending budget and locked down every penny so that we had virtually no cash available. I had to ask for money, I had to ask to buy things, I had to ask to get groceries. I had to ask his permission. It was just another way that he grabbed and maintained control over me and made me terrified of breaking his rules for fear of his consequences. I could not fight back because I was just no match for him. I was never any match for him. We are never any match for them. We are human. They are a different breed all their own.

———————

As I look back on her – the me that I was – I feel heartache, pain, and frustration for and with the girl and then woman I was. There is a distance now between us, a distance borne of my newfound strength and independence; of my commitment to taking my life back. And yet, she is a part of me, and so I acknowledge her for her sake and for yours – so that you may see yourself in her journey and learn from it; so, you might avoid the situation in which she found herself; and so that, if you are in the midst of it, you find solace in knowing she was there, too – and that I am now she, and she is free.

If I could go back in time, there are so many things that I know now I would warn her about. But the one thing I wish I really could affect is the mistake that I know she is about to make during her forty-first year. I watch her every day in sadness and in fear as time almost stands still. I know what she is about to do, and there is no stopping her now. She will make the mistake of her life, and she will pay dearly for it.

I head to my laptop with an urgency that could push a truck through a brick wall. This is the moment. This is why I am here. This is why I am doing this. This is what I am trying to warn you about. Please, if you ever hear one thing I am saying, please if you ever read a word, read this: MAKE A PLAN WITH THE PROFESSIONALS BEFORE YOU LEAVE.

Slow and Steady Wins the Race

"Slow and steady wins the race." It's my favorite quote. I say it all the time, I share it with friends and family, and I even once got it inside of a fortune cookie! That fortune is still inside of my wallet sixteen years later. It's something I truly believe in. I held onto it for years while I desperately lived inside a house and a life that tortured me. It was a beacon of hope that something, somehow would someday change. But what does it mean?

This quote comes to us from the famous story "The Tortoise and the Hare," one of Aesop's Fables. If you have kids you may have read it to them, or you may even remember it from your own childhood. It you think about it, this fable can change your life and change your life plan today. Please consider this. The story is about two highly unequal partners, a rabbit (the hare) and a turtle (the tortoise). The rabbit is mocking the turtle for being so slow that he challenges it to a race. The rabbit is so sure that he will win the race that he takes off like lightning, gets far ahead, and then takes a nap under a tree, all the while laughing at the slow and plodding turtle. So, what does the turtle do? The turtle just keeps going because it knows that if it just keeps taking one step at a time as fast as it can, it will eventually cross the finish line. By the time the rabbit wakes up from his nap the turtle is crossing the finish line and has won the race. The rabbit is furious and in disbelief. What just happened? The turtle HAD A PLAN. The rabbit never saw it coming.

Oh, I bet you see where I am going with this don't you? So often, abusers have classic narcissistic personalities. According to the Mayo Clinic, people with narcissistic personality disorder, "...come across as conceited, boastful or pretentious...often monopolize conversations...belittle or look down on people [they] perceive as inferior." It goes on to explain that the root cause of this behavior is that the person "may have secret feelings of insecurity, shame, vulnerability and humiliation. To feel better, [they] may react with rage or contempt and try to belittle the other person to make [themselves] appear superior."

Anyone just read their life story here? It sure was mine. I was the tortoise for over twenty years. I was slow and plodding. He was quick and always believed that he would get there first. So I am showing you something very big today. I am showing you HOW TO WIN THE RACE. Because you know what? You can. I did, so you can, too. Here's how.

Even though abusers wear us down, we have to remember who we were before it started. You have to go back to a time when you were a complete and shiny bubble full of air and floating in your life. Think of that time and tell yourself, "I can be that person again, it's just a short plan away." It is true. Then you have to do something very important. You have to play on your strengths and use them to your advantage. He sees you as weak and unable to accomplish anything? Perfect! Don't change a thing. Stay right there. This is what the turtle did. The turtle didn't shout out, "Hey jerk! While you're sleeping I am going to win the race!" What would have happened if he did? The rabbit would have seen the plan, foregone his nap, and crossed the finish line. He would have made the turtle pay for it dearly and then peacefully went to sleep under the tree. Don't share your plan. Just make one.

So what do you do? Start by getting to a place where you are safe. Use a phone or computer that is not yours that cannot be monitored. Call THE NATIONAL DOMESTIC VIOLENCE HOTLINE or go to thehotline.org and ask them how to start your plan for getting out. Then, very slowly, you put one foot in front of the other and you begin to plan your race. You never talk about it. You never act as if anything has changed. You just keep your head down and follow the plan that you make. When he mocks you, then you take it. When he taunts you, you accept it. All the while you say in your head, "Slow and steady wins the race," and you picture yourself in a safe place. You follow your plan and you do not deviate. Remember, the turtle was smart because it followed the plan. The rabbit lost because he knew he would win. Don't think you will win just because you are smart. That is when you will lose.

If you think about one thing today, please think about this: SLOW AND STEADY WINS THE RACE. You can do this. Just make your plan. I'm on the sidelines, I'm in the bleachers, I'm at your race, and I'm rooting you on. I'm your biggest fan.

Remember this: STRENGTH + SUPPORT + PLAN = FREEDOM. You can do this.

It's so tempting once you know that you want to leave, to just want to leave right then. It probably feels like it's taken forever to make your decision, so once you do you're ready to go! You've been told that you are worthless one too many times. You've been frightened to your core one too many times. And you've been told how weak you are one too many times. But the crazy thing about domestic abuse victims is that we are not weak. In fact, quite the opposite. Who else can live a life of abuse and get out of bed every day? Who else can continue to raise children, show up at work, show up for life, and just keep living?

Recognize that strength and use it to your advantage. It costs you nothing to let him think he is winning while he is not.

One caveat: If you truly feel your life or the lives of your children are in danger, leave immediately and get help.

I see her at age 28 getting ready to go to work that morning. She is exhausted from what he has put her through the night before and trying desperately to get ready and be on time. She races in, pushing the speed limit all the way, knowing what will happen to her if she gets a speeding ticket, so she is watching her speedometer like a hawk the entire time.

She was told the day before that management had an important meeting this morning and that they all must be there on time. They are waiting for someone who is running late who finally stumbles in looking flustered and exclaims, "Oh my gosh, I am having the worst day! I got a flat tire on the way to work and I had to wait 45 minutes for the tow truck to arrive. I never thought I would make it here, thanks for waiting for me, sorry!" *Really?* She thinks to herself. *That's a bad day?* She thinks about this for a minute. I suppose that would be a bad day for someone who is living a normal life.

But she thinks about what it has taken her to get here on time and imagines what it would be like if she turned to everyone and said what she was thinking at that moment: *Oh my gosh, I am having the worst day too! Last night my husband yelled at me for forty-five minutes because he couldn't find the remote control and he was sure I threw it away when I was cleaning our living room. Then he looked inside the trash and saw that I had used another roll of toilet paper. Then he yelled at me for using too many rolls of toilet paper again this week and said I could only have one more to get through the rest of the week. He was so angry so I tried to leave the room, but he followed me to the next room. He then asked me if I had gotten the mail. I got sick to my stomach because I had forgotten. He told me to stay there with a look that made me know not to move. He stormed out and got the mail. He came back in, opened the mail in front of me, and I held my breath because I saw that our credit card bill was in there. He then spent two hours reviewing every purchase I made, asking why I spent so much on groceries, what I bought at the drugstore, what exactly I had bought at the office supply store, if our company was going to pay me back, if I had submitted an expense report, when I would get the check back, that I had better give him the check and not spend it on myself, and why I had bought a new outfit for work.*

I tried to leave the room, but he wouldn't let me. He said I always tried to leave and that is why we never accomplished anything. I started to sweat and my hands started shaking. He noticed and asked me why I was sick again. By the time I got to bed it was after midnight. This morning I put on the new outfit I bought for work today and he told me I looked like 'a flower dressed to go to Las Vegas.' I'm not sure what that meant, but I don't feel great about what I'm wearing right now and you all know I'm making that huge presentation to our partners this afternoon. I'm wondering if I have time to go to the mall and buy something else during my lunch break, but then I'll have to get yelled at again when the credit card bill comes next month. I guess it could have been worse. My haircut wasn't on the bill, so I won't have to deal with that until next month. He told me to go to the cheap place in the mall where they only cut kid's hair, but they keep chopping my hair too short and he yells at me for having short hair, so I went to the real salon. That is going to be a bad night.

"Susan? You going to join us?" she hears her boss ask. "Oh, yes of course," she answers as she takes her seat and turns her attention to her work. They have no idea what her real life is like. They rely on her, and she delivers every single time. They just have no idea.

We become masterful actors, abuse victims. We hide from the world what we don't want them to see. We hide from ourselves what we don't want to face. And we hide from our abusers the pain and anguish they cause us because we know how much they enjoy it. But what about those days when we cry so hard that we hide in our bathrooms or our closets or our cars and say to ourselves that we just can't take it one moment longer. What about those days where we know that we are staring our destiny right in the eye if we stay here? Is this your life? Do you know what I mean when I tell you that you are not alone? This was my life. YOU ARE NOT ALONE.

Tears slowly slide down my face as I publish this blog because it hurts so much to remember all of the details of what he put me through. When I say I hate going back, I mean it, I hate going back. I hate remembering those days, I hate remembering his words, I hate remembering what I hid, how it hurt, how I crumbled and nearly broke so many times. And it hurts to think that you could be going through this now, or you did, or you one day might. No one ever said taking this journey would be easy. And on a day like today I'm not feeling the strength and power surge through my body as much as I am feeling the old and familiar pain just course through me as I remember what my life was and what happened to me. Then I take a deep breath, I look around the room, I see my freedom right in front of me, and I remember why I am here. I am here for you. I was the one in four. Now you are, or you were, or you one day might be. Let's change that together. Let's change that forever.

7

Three Times a Lady

> WARNING SIGN OF DOMESTIC ABUSE:
> Controls who you see, where you go, or what you do,
> or prevents you from working or attending school

Part of what kept me going, of what probably keeps a lot of abuse victims going, is the persona we present to the world. In my case, I was a successful business executive – successful enough to buy and maintain a beautiful home. Then I became a mother, a good mother, to two wonderful boys. I was smart, accomplished, attractive – a woman who could hold her own. That was who most people saw, and so long as that was who *they* were seeing, I could pretend to be her at least part of the time. When not being assaulted by him, I could pretend my life was good. But as his control grew, as his fixation on me grew, my pretend time shrank. It was only a matter of time before a perfect storm would ensue.

When I think about the level of control that he gained over me and how he basically dictated my every move, it is astounding to me. He did this by using two primary tools: fear and intimidation. He knew what I was afraid of: upsetting our children, embarrassing our family, revealing our secret of abuse, and looking weak to others who considered me to be a strong person who had accomplished so much. And of course, he knew I was afraid of him. He knew how to intimidate me: by going after our children if I would not comply; by embarrassing me out in public to give me a taste of just what he would do if I did not follow his orders, which would of course reveal our secret of abuse and cause me to act strange and show the world that I was not Super Woman after all. He has this all tied together in a perfect, neat, little package. The people-pleaser, the world-pleaser, who cared too much and put everyone else first, was too worried about everything to ever stand up for herself, especially if doing so would implode her carefully-constructed illusions. He had me exactly where he wanted me.

When we were out in public he would test me often. He would ask me to do something that he knew I did not want to do. I would very quietly deny his request. As loudly as he possibly could he would then shout, "WHAT? WHAT DID YOU SAY? I CANNOT HEAR YOU, IT IS VERY LOUD IN HERE." And wherever we were, people would stop what they were doing to stare at us because we had just become a public spectacle. He played on all of my fears at once, and I would immediately comply with him and do what he wanted. If he went too forceful, he would cause a panic attack and I would end up shaking, sweating, and trying to regain my composure while feeling faint and trying to watch over our babies. He had me cornered and was using my own weaknesses against me. It was brutal, it was toxic, it was pure evil, and he did it almost every time we left the house. The quieter the environment – a restaurant, the grocery store, a book store or library, or any place that he did not want to be in – the louder he was. This started a whole new phobia for me; I started to become afraid to leave my house. If he embarrassed me at home, and I went into full meltdown, at least I was embarrassed in my own home. Being embarrassed like that in public was just becoming too much for me to handle.

Because of this whole new level of control that he had over me, it was easy for him to tell me not to go out with certain people, or go to certain places, or attempt to join groups, or better myself in any way. If I did go out, he would try to come along; and I already knew what he would do to me when he got there. He had full control over me, and I was changing into a person that could not control when she turned into a flaming hot puddle of sweat for the whole world to watch. It was like a volcanic meltdown. I once remember a woman looking at me and saying, "Wow, you look way too young to be having a hot flash," and I was mortified to my core. How do you explain to someone that you are having a panic attack when you can barely breathe, barely stand up straight, barely speak, and don't want to admit to anyone what is happening anyway? The fear of having these attacks would even spark an attack. The fear of the fear would often cause me to stay home and miss events or not see my friends because I could no longer hide my problems and I could not admit to them either. I was in a horrible place, and I had no idea how to get out. My life was becoming more like a solitary confinement prison every day, and my warden lived at home with me 24/7 because he didn't work. I had one final chance to get out and take a stab at surviving this, and I somehow gathered the strength and took a shot at it.

———————

I see her at forty-one years old. She does not know it yet, but this will be the defining year of her life. She looks like she is well into her fifties. She has recovered from her fall down the stairs, but she walks with a gentle limp as her right foot does the rest of its healing. More of her body was broken than she had originally thought from the fall, and she has much work to do in physical therapy. She has gained weight and doesn't yet realize just how much. She knows that her clothes do not fit, so she buys a few new pairs of jeans and manages with tops that she can still squeeze into.

Her body feels weak and broken, and she doesn't know what is happening to her. She makes a mental note to go see a doctor and then pushes it aside as she knows her focus has to remain on getting strong enough to leave and not worrying about much more. Her gut instinct just keeps telling her to get physically strong as quickly as possible and let everything else wait.

She is working in the PTA, building a larger network every day, and making stronger ties as she becomes more visible and more integral to her community. She is managing budgets, planning events, and making changes that will positively impact her children's enrichment and education. Somehow, she instinctively knows that she is slowly weaving her own lifeline, and her focus remains laser-like as she gets out of bed each day and divides her free time between physical therapy and working at the school.

As much as she is accomplishing in the outside world, I see her come home each afternoon in fear. She walks in quietly, begins cooking quietly, and helps the boys with their homework quietly when they come home from school. It's almost as if she hopes he will forget that she is alive and maybe, just maybe, she will make it through a day without being abused. She is tiptoeing through her home-life in an effort not to make an imprint, not to rub up against life or, heaven forbid, create a spark. She lives her life with so much fear that even a whisper that is uttered too loudly can now set off a panic attack: someone walking up too quickly behind her without her noticing, or anyone taking her off guard sends her reeling to a place that is hard, far too hard, to come back from.

I see this unfold as if I'm watching a television drama that I can't take my eyes off of. The balance of power is gently shifting, and he can feel it. She is getting smarter about how and where to spend her time and energy when the children are at school, and he is growing more furious by the minute. He is threatening her more, trying harder to intimidate her, and scaring her in every way possible. She, in turn, just bides her time until she can leave her home the next day and escape to the safety of the school where she is in charge of a group that welcomes her, loves her, and wants her help. It is a place that makes her feel safe, reminds her that she is alive, worth something, and still able to contribute to the world outside of her home. They feed the soul that was dying inside of her, they recharge the battery that is almost dead, and with this validation, she can feel the life slowly building from within.

And so, her confidence starts to build. At night when he calls her dumb, worthless, and incompetent she is finding it harder to believe because that is not what the others are saying. He has no proof of it. But she has proof that her hard work is making a difference in her other world. She starts to see, for the first time in many years, that he may just possibly be wrong. He notices the difference in her and he is in a rage. She sees him fretting all the time now. She notices that he is moodier than ever. He sulks more. He hurls even more insults. She does not respond. She simply walks away because she no longer believes him. Yes, the balance in power is definitely starting to shift. Even while she revels in the knowledge, she knows that this is not going to end well.

———————

I see her on that cloudy Saturday morning when he finally hits his breaking point. The boys are happily playing their new video game together, and he sees an opportunity to get her alone and confront her without them hearing him. For as much as he abused her, he was masterful at being scary when their boys were not around, and masterful at threatening her right in front of them, too, in ways that he could get away with because they did not understand. At first, they were so little they were blind to it. This was just dad and mom. It was all they knew. And she never changed her expression when he acted out, so they never saw her fear. It was the ultimate sacrifice of love and kindness to her boys, and it took the ultimate in self-control and discipline on her part not to react.

But that one cloudy Saturday morning will forever live in her memory, a morning when he saw an opportunity to get her away from the children and give her all he had. In front of the boys, he asked gently to speak with her privately, and she could not say no. She felt fear course through her body and a lump form in her throat as he walked her down the hall into his home office. She hated this room! He would sit behind his desk like a school principal, and he would seat her in the chair in front of his desk like the errant child that had been sent to his office. He would stare down over her, chastise her, berate her, come at her with everything he had, and she would cower in fear, and bide her time until she could escape. She knew what was coming, and she had known for a long while that it would be coming. Here it was.

"It's me or the PTA, and you better pick one right now!" he spits at her with fury on his face and an inferno of hate spilling from his eyes, so hot that she can feel the burn on her skin from across his desk. He leans forward in rage, using every tool in his arsenal to scare, intimidate, and control her. The vein is throbbing in his forehead and his eyes are boring into her. He expects her to jump and shrink back as she would normally do, apologize, make it right, say something to soften the moment. But instead she studies his face and sees everything for the first time as if someone has just put glasses on her eyes that clear not just her vision but her mind, too. She is stunned to hear the words simply fall out of her mouth, "I don't think you are going to like my answer."

———————

For years people will ask me why twenty years? I met him when I was 21 and I left when I was 41. Why? Well I can't tell you why because I am still figuring out the why for myself. But in that one singular moment so much flashed before my eyes. So many years of pain, so many years of humiliation and torment, so many years of lost friends, opportunities, adventures, estrangement from family, and job opportunities turned down. But on that one cloudy Saturday morning something finally happened. I had the recognition that I was still worth something in the world, and I decided this one final time he wasn't going to throw a roadblock and I wasn't giving up on me.

Twenty years. Did I love him? Of course. Did I believe him when he said he would change? Of course. This is a very large part of the cycle of abuse. Good days and bad days. Fun times and bad times. Glorious days with your children and thousands of nights crying yourself to sleep. Crawling out on a limb and trying to explain how badly he is hurting you, telling him that you will leave if he doesn't stop, he tells you he understands and you believe him! You believe him! He'll change! He says he'll change! And you're so happy that he will change because that is all you ever wanted. You want the kind man back that you fell in love with. You want him back. Then you wake up the next day with the new man. The new man that you didn't fall in love with, that you didn't marry, and your heart breaks all over again. This is the cycle of abuse and it never stops. If you think it will stop I am here to tell you, after twenty years, that it will not stop.

And there are so many more factors that complicate our lives if we are being abused. So many of us are raised to be ladies, people-pleasers; and ladies just don't make trouble. Because ladies are here to make our men happy and raise our children. This is a large problem in the cycle of abuse. If we are not raised to stand up for ourselves, if we are not taught to challenge things when they do not seem right, then we are prime targets for abusers. We are easily groomed. Despite any obvious strengths, we have a flaw that renders us vulnerable. We are weak and we don't know it. If we are not educated as to what abuse is and is not, then how do we know it when it happens to us? And if we are not taught that we are better than that – and who would think that someone would need to tell us that, but they do – we may simply sit there and take it, hoping that things will change and get better because they tell us that they will change and we believe them!

And where did this lady fit in anyway? This lady who set her family up financially for the rest of their lives – including her abusive husband – from her career. This lady who made and broke record after record in her life and amazed everyone around her. Where did this lady fit in? She didn't. And so, she got lost in an endless cycle of abuse because no one ever told her, and it occurred to her way too late that it was ok not to fit in. It was ok to be a leader, and it was ok not to please everyone all of the time. It just occurred to her way too late. Twenty years too late because no one had ever told her otherwise. Because they didn't think they needed to.

If you are twenty-one, if you are a parent of a young woman, or if you are anyone that could be a one in four, this one is really and truly for you. Because the truth is, love should be a gentle and safe place to rest your head and your heart in life. There shouldn't be any sparks in love, not the kind that burn. Not the kind that start fires. Not the kind that leave scars that may never heal.

Three Times a Lady...

When I was a little girl my parents taught me all about manners, being polite, and "acting like a lady." I was raised in a loving home with my brother, my sister, and our dog. There was a lot of love to give and share. But the notion of saying please and thank-you, waiting your turn, not interrupting, not breaking our rules, not cheating, stealing, or hurting anyone's feelings on purpose were taught to us very clearly. I was raised to respect others, and my family respected others, so we lived peacefully together. When you leave a world like that, and enter one where someone else is not behaving the same way, that is where you run into problems. You are vulnerable to abuse; you never see it coming because you have no idea what it looks like. And if no one has ever warned you to watch out for it, well you're as good as gone.

If you always show up as a lady, and one day showing up that way means you are defenseless in a world that you do not understand, the problems begin. Peace is no match for destruction. I showed up as a lady when I met my husband. I was kind, gentle, and young. I was respectful of him and his feelings. I followed his rules,

I didn't lie, cheat, or steal, and I certainly did not hurt his feelings. That is the way I was raised, and because of that I was never any match for him.

Good people take responsibility for their actions and for the way their actions impact others. They show up. I showed up again when I became a mom. Dealing with the struggles and the pain at home and somehow thinking we could make this work and that things would change, that he would do what he said he would do, that he "would stop", was the world I lived in. Sound familiar? I was living in a rational world in which people made agreements to change behaviors and when adults said things would change, then things would change. What I learned is that there is nothing rational nor normal or adult-like about domestic abuse. It never makes sense.

The third time I showed up as a lady was the last year of my marriage, but this time I was barely recognizable. Broken then healed, health failing in every direction, hair falling out, I was, quite literally, falling to pieces. The abuse was at an all-time high and the insults just kept coming from my husband. I had also put on weight from the stress of the situation and the medications that the doctors were using to try and stabilize me. I would walk into the room to hear things like: "I just looked up at your face across the room and it scared me. It's huge!" "Do you even fit in your clothes anymore?" "What's wrong with you? Why have you gained so much weight?" "Why are you always tired?" "Why are you always sick?" I was mortified. I was in a very bad situation but I was, after all, a lady, and I was trying to keep it together with grace and dignity.

One day I was driving home and I was talking to a friend. For one moment in time I stopped being a lady, forgot my manners, and blurted out something rude about how bad my marriage was without even thinking. The phone went silent and I thought we had been disconnected. Then I heard this, "I would never let anyone treat me that way. You don't deserve that." I was just pulling into my neighborhood and my eyes filled with tears. The road started to blur in front of me and I pulled over to the curb. Now I was speechless. This person was right. I didn't deserve any of this. Why in the world did I ever think that I did? Such a simple statement but it changed everything. "You do everything for everyone," the friend continued, "What are you doing for you?" *What are you doing for you, lady?*

For the next several months every time I heard an insult I silently said in my head, "I don't deserve this," and then I moved on. Every time I was called fat, or stupid, or incompetent, or lazy, or not a good mother, or whatever else came my way, I simply said to myself, "I don't deserve this." For me that statement started to generate inner strength and the clarity to see things for what they were. I did not deserve to be abused like this. How had I let this go on for so long?

That summer we all gathered for my mom's birthday like we did every year. My whole family was around one table. It was a lunch I always dreaded because I was in fear of what my husband would say. True to form, he managed to insult most of my family, make everyone uncomfortable, and leave me feeling shamed and embarrassed. Right as we were getting up to leave the voice came back in my head and I heard it so loud and so clear, "I DON'T DESERVE THIS." I decided right then and there that it would be the last birthday lunch that my husband would ever attend with my family. The next day I told him I wanted a divorce.

Walking out that summer I was in pretty bad shape! I was on so many prescription medications that I needed a pill box to keep me organized. It dawned on me in that moment that I had been such a lady, and an endless people-pleaser, that I forgot something. I forgot to show up for me. I showed up for my children, I showed up for my family, I showed up for my friends, and I showed up for my community. What was I doing for me? The road from here was not an easy one. I made mistakes. I announced my divorce without a plan for my safety. I announced my divorce without a plan period. In the end that cost me and it hurt me. That is the driving force behind this blog. I want to help you avoid the mistakes I made.

What we live through as SODAs™, unfortunately, does not get erased as we move forward through life. But the good news is that we move further away from it every day. We instinctively learn what we will and will not put up with in life, and we react accordingly. This time we see things coming because it is a life lesson that stays with us forever. I now see potentially dangerous situations from a mile away, and I simply turn and walk in another direction. You can get here, too. I know you may not see it today because I didn't see it that day, either. So, just in case you need the friend that I needed that day, I will now tell you the same. If you are living a life of domestic abuse: "YOU DON'T DESERVE THIS."

Remember this: STRENGTH + SUPPORT + PLAN = FREEDOM. You can do this.

So many thoughts continue to swirl through my head as I finish this blog. I see the pieces of the puzzle of my life start to connect, and I realize that my purpose is really so clear. I stayed for twenty years, and that is truly a tragic tale. But because of what happened to me, I have a lot of knowledge to share with you that could help you get out so much sooner. In fact, my knowledge may help keep you from ever becoming vulnerable at all.

If you're someone who has also stayed for twenty years, or almost twenty, or more than twenty, or just altogether too long, then I am here to tell you that there is no shame in getting stuck. Abuse is an insidious whirlpool. It is emotional quicksand. It sucks us in even as we try to move forward.

Another truth is that domestic abuse will hurt forever. We can never truly leave it behind. It changes who we are, it changes who we were, and it definitely changes who we will become. But it also gives us a very rare opportunity, the chance and choice to grab back a good life. So, it really doesn't matter how long you stayed or why it happened to you. It just matters that you know that you can still reclaim a good life. The power is in leaving. Don't look back, look forward. I did and I am making it work. You absolutely can too.

I feel a renewed sense of hope when I publish this blog. I need to warn you, I need to warn everyone. I have so much to warn you about and so much to help you with. Don't please others and put yourself last. Don't forget to watch out for your safety and get this now: there is zero shame in asking for help when you need it. There is still so much we need to discuss! I close my laptop and start thinking about this, and I know exactly what we need to do next. I know I won't sleep tonight as thoughts are already forming in my mind.

8
It's Not a Dream

(**WARNING SIGN OF DOMESTIC ABUSE:**
Looks at you or acts in ways that scare you or
intimidates you with guns, knives, or other weapons)

I learned something very dangerous about domestic abuse as I neared the end of my marriage. And I didn't learn it from hearing it on the news one night, or from reading it in a magazine where someone was trying to warn me. I learned it, sadly, from the story of my own life. And when I think about it now it makes so much sense I don't know how I missed it, I can only think that I was so close to the situation that there was just no way to see it. And I didn't know. I simply did not know.

If domestic abusers gain joy and pleasure from controlling their victims, what happens when their victims finally declare a new day? What happens when we decide that we have had enough and that we are leaving? I didn't know then, but I can tell you now: the first 24 hours after you leave are the most dangerous; up to 75% of people who flee their abusers are then murdered by them.

In my case, I watched him come undone screw-by-screw and piece-by-piece, as if someone were taking a robot apart. I no longer saw him as human, and he definitely wasn't acting that way. I should have been more scared. I should have been more aware. I should have done a million things differently. Instead I got lost in the thrill and excitement of the fact that I was about to break free, and I completely forgot who I was breaking free from.

I see her as a little girl. She is seven years old and they are standing on a dock at the beach in New Jersey. Her dad has just given her a sparkler and he is about to light it. "Daddy!" she yells, "I'm scared! It's going to hurt me!"

"No," he smiles, "It won't hurt you. You'll love it, it's so pretty." He leans over and lights the sparkler and she is at once both thrilled and terrified. "Daddy!" she yells, "Daddy help!" and he leans over with a gentle smile and puts his hand over hers. They hold the sparkler together and watch the beautiful beams of light shoot out in every direction.

"See?" he says, "It won't hurt you. Just don't touch the red part where it's hot." She looks at the fiery lights shooting in all directions and feels joy and wonder. She is safe with her daddy, and she is holding something beautiful in her hand, something with a life all its own. Hand over hand they had managed the sparks. Watched the beauty and avoided the burn. Love should always shine that way, and love should never be dangerous. She loved her daddy so much, and he always kept her safe and knew just what to do to protect her. Together they always had sparks of love. The kind of sparks that they were holding together: bright, colorful, safe, beautiful.

I see her, now forty-one years old, health failing, broken and battered. She is standing by the beach again. This time she has fled her home to get away from him right after she has told him that she wants a divorce. The beach is a place where she feels safe, and she and her children and mother have come here while she lets him cool down. With him, sparks too, have always flown. He is a piece of flint that does not need another to ignite. Life is his other piece of flint. He simply has to move through space and time and he creates sparks all on his own.

This is not his wonder. This is his curse. Never was this a true spark of love. This was a spark of hope that she so desperately wanted to hold in her hand and feel and see something magical again. To tell him that she was afraid, and to have him put his hand over hers and tell her that everything would be ok. But this was never meant to be and would never happen. For he was a spark all his own and no matter where she touched him he was red hot, and so with every touch she would be burned.

I see her standing on that beach and I know she will never be the same. It is her birthday and it is the most horrible birthday she has ever had. It started out in her home and now here she was standing by the ocean a few hundred miles away trying to process what she had just been through. The nightmare had gotten worse. How in the world could her nightmare of a life get even worse? She was taking deep breaths of the fresh salt air and trying to get her breathing to slow down. She was trying to get her composure so she could turn and smile and tell her boys that everything would be ok.

She had woken up that morning and thrown open her bedroom doors to gather the boys and head to the beach to celebrate her birthday. It was a family tradition and they went every year, only this year would be a little different. The boys did not know it yet, but this year they were going without their dad. She had told him that she wanted a divorce, and they were going to tell the children together this morning. Then she was going to take them to the beach with her mother for a week while things calmed down a bit. They would return home and make a plan to go from there. This was all happening very quickly, so she was looking forward to getting to a safe place, a place that she knew very well, and to giving him some time alone, too. She needed to know that there would be a few hundred miles between them. She needed to know that she would lock a bedroom door that night that could not be unlocked, and she needed to know that for the first time in several months she would get a normal night of sleep.

Pain and anguish cross two little faces as they meet her at the door and announce that "Daddy says you are sending him away to live in a little room all by himself and we will never see him again." Her knees start to buckle as she reels with the understanding of what he has just done. He has told the boys of their divorce without her and in a way that is so cruel that he has sent them into a total panic. In that moment, he showed her that there was nothing he would not do to get to her, and collateral damage was of no concern to him – even if that collateral damage was their sons. With superhuman strength and speed she regains her composure and reassures these little people that no one is going anywhere and that they will have two parents for life. They are pleased with the news and go off to play a game of catch with their football. Neither wanting nor caring to control her furor, she walks right up to him and does something she has never done in her life: she rages one inch from his face about what he has just done. She fears nothing, sees nothing, knows nothing but pure white anger and hatred. The monster has made a monster, if only for just a moment. She tells him if he ever does anything like that again, she will make sure that he pays for it. She gathers the children and her mother and they leave for the beach.

———————

It sounds like I found my footing that morning and became a force to be reckoned with. Well, let me tell you something very clearly right now. You don't confront an abuser like that EVER. What I basically did was refuel his gas tank with premium gasoline. I gave him what he wanted. I gave him a brand-new reason to fight, to hate, and to slaughter. This was the beginning of my failings for not having a plan. This was the beginning of me doing every single thing wrong because I didn't ask a professional how to escape abuse without getting hurt or killed. This was where I went so wrong that there would be no coming back. And in the end, I paid a high price for my mistakes.

Leaving my marriage was the most terrifying thing I have ever done in my life. It took every ounce of strength, courage, and a backbone that I didn't know was still in there. I announced to him, in a moment of bravery, that he wouldn't like my choice between him and the PTA, but I didn't have a plan. I just knew I couldn't take it one more moment, and I broke.

The words hung in the air like bullets you see in a movie that move in slow motion so you can follow their path. They moved slowly towards him until they hit. He sat there in a quiet rage and I knew that I had to continue right then or I never would. I mustered the strength and courage and quietly announced, "I want a divorce."

He said nothing as he stared at me, and so I took that moment to get myself out of that office before anything else could happen.

I was terrified. I ran back to find the children happily playing their video game, and I sat next to them while thoughts were racing through my mind at the speed of light.

What in the world was I going to do next? I knew with every instinct in my body that I had to get out of there as soon as possible, so I called my mother and told her what had happened. She packed a suitcase and headed straight to my home, and we took the boys and left for the beach to get away from him so he could cool down.

I didn't think through what would happen next as I was taking this one step at a time and living in pure survival mode. In my mind, it was over and he was ok with it. Why did I ever think that? I have no idea. I suppose when someone tells you how much they hate you and how everything is wrong with you for twenty years, you start to think that they will be pretty happy if you finally get the nerve to leave. What I know now is that the exact opposite is true.

If someone is living to control you and your every move and you break free, break the cycle of abuse, show independence in any way, you have thrown down a gauntlet larger than life itself. And this is what I had just done. Only I didn't know it because for all the schooling I had, somehow, I missed Abuse 101 and had no idea what was going on in my own life. For someone who was always that perfect student, I had so much to learn about the psychology of abuse.

I had just committed the single most dangerous act of an abuse victim. I had announced my leaving without a plan for my own safety. I simply stayed away from home for a week and then came back. Here, you will see, is where it all starts to unravel. Here is where I made mistake after mistake, not knowing any better, unable to do any better, and learning the painful lessons of a lifetime.

This blog, a particularly difficult one, I purposely leave as long as possible before I write because it is here that my life went from the daily abuse that we hide behind closed doors to the kind of abuse about which you write books, the kind of abuse that people then want to make into movies. It is here that he got bold, it is here that he got bigger, it is here that he stopped caring about people seeing who he truly was because his eye was on his prize, me, and he was losing her.

He set traps that are beyond imagination. He enlisted teams of people to help him. He would stop at nothing to "get me" but what did "getting me" mean? To him it was pure revenge for my leaving, a revenge that lives and breathes to this day. It is here that he began to falter, for his puppet had cut the strings.

He violated my trust, he invaded my privacy, and he entered the confines of my mind in order to exact a plan so ugly and vicious that no sane person could ever see it coming. He crossed the lines of reason and he broke the written laws that govern our society, and all of this without a care in the world. Rules never meant anything to him. Rules were for other people. Rules were for the weak. Rules were for the "little," and he was big and he was powerful and he was strong.

It's Not a Dream...

There are two very famous movies that I think about often as I continue my journey of recovery from domestic abuse. One I saw as an innocent child on a lovely Sunday afternoon with my family: "E.T. the Extra-Terrestrial." The second I saw as an adult who was not so innocent: "Gaslight," on a dark Sunday evening, alone.

Sometimes I look back and I honestly can't believe some of what I have been through. I think it could be a crazy dream. A dream where an adorable alien came down from another planet, showed me that love is real with his heartlight, took me on a ride towards the moon, then dropped me off in bed and forced me to wake up only to realize that I was not being loved, that instead I was being tortured. It's like a crazy mashup of these two movies somehow became my life. If anything actually did rub off on me from these movies other than the importance of love in our lives it would be "expect the unexpected," or "believe the impossible to be possible." I say this for a very important reason.

"Gaslight" has become a movie that is very important for abuse victims to be aware of. In it, a man is trying to convince his wife that she is crazy. He plays tricks on her and isolates her in their home. When she sees the gaslight flickering in her room at night, he tells her that it is not happening and she is seeing things. There is an actual term borne from this movie called "gaslighting", meaning to do something to someone to make them think that they are crazy when indeed they are not.

None of us plan to marry someone who will intentionally gaslight us. Do you think I would have done this? Of course not! But things do happen that we didn't see coming, as happened to me. Until I remembered one thing that I was lucky enough not to have forgotten: Turn on your heartlight and turn off that gaslight because the knob is in your hands and you are still in control here.

After I fell down the stairs, my husband had planted video cameras throughout our home. I did not know about the cameras. He was watching my every move and listening to my every word. When I sought legal counsel for our divorce, he knew. When I asked my friends for advice, he knew. He could hear every single word I said all day long.

And then he took it a diabolical step further. He put a tracking device on my car. At first, I didn't know how he would show up at a place where I was going before I could get there. It was haunting. Or I would take the boys to lunch and one of his friends would be sitting at the next table just coincidentally, staring us down during the entire meal just to make us uncomfortable.

He was "gaslighting" me and guess what? It got worse from there! He hired Private Investigators to follow me everywhere like trained thugs. This one was easier to figure out because I could see them following me and taking pictures. I felt like I was in the middle of a bad television movie. One of those movies where the wife usually gets killed in the last five minutes and the husband gets away with her murder.

My husband violated a Federal Wiretapping law by illegally audiotaping my every word for all of those months. Yet, when we tried to tell the court system, they simply didn't care. They said that that law was really there for important people like politicians and celebrities. Spouses do this all the time to one another, and they just don't have the time to prosecute these cases.

My intention of taking this public is to ensure that courts do take this more seriously because it was an illegal invasion of privacy and one that is beyond unacceptable to anyone at any level. And if it could happen to me, it could happen to any of us.

It was an illegal invasion of my privacy and a direct threat to my safety, and the justice system did not protect me. I had Private Investigators, an intensely driven husband, his amped up group of friends, and his hired bodyguards following me everywhere I went and tracking my every move. It's a wonder that this didn't escalate to something even uglier. It's a wonder that I made it out safely. It's a wonder that I made it out SANELY.

So, there are two things that are going on here and both really end up being equally important. Gaslighting: When things don't look and sound normal to you, trust your instincts because they probably are not. If you think someone is following you then they might be. If you think they're listening to you then they probably are. If you think they're going through your phone or computer I would bet my life on it. It's not hard to get experts to help you protect yourself. I highly recommend it. Follow the law and let the law help you. Don't attempt this on your own.

Heartlight: You have to keep it turned on to remember who you are at all times. You are the good, kind, and honest one, so stay up on that high road where you belong at all times. Do not go down and meet them in the gutter because they belong down there and you do not. It will never serve you well. You are the person who accidentally fell in love with someone who is out to hurt you. Don't turn off your heartlight because people can use it to find you when all else goes wrong. Keep shining bright, and keep telling everyone where you are going and who you are with. And, by all means, turn your real GPS tracking on your phone at all times and go straight to the police station if you think you are in danger.

None of this is ever a joke. Only you decide when you float, if your burst your own bubble, or if you remain trapped forever. No one does that to a SODA™ but a SODA™. Pick your flavor, make your choice, press that button. It's your dollar.

Remember this: STRENGTH + SUPPORT + PLAN = FREEDOM. You can do this.

My life during this time is very hard to reflect back on because it is so painful, and to this day I still feel so violated and have developed many trust issues as a result. Emotional rape. It's the best possible way I can describe it. I was emotionally violated by my own husband, and it made me feel dirty and disgusting and frightened. It brought me to a place lower than I could imagine because I thought I was already living on the bottom.

Picture yourself having a phone call with your best friend. Now, imagine someone comes into the room and says, "I am going to videotape your phone call, go ahead and continue." Wouldn't you act differently? Choose different words? Edit your content? Of course you would. I never had that choice, in the safety and privacy of my own home, in my bathroom, in my closet, and in my own bedroom. And to be recorded while speaking to my divorce attorney about our plan for my divorce? Does it get more personal than that? What he did to me with the information he obtained from the hidden cameras and tracking devices was truly criminal in and of itself. He would mention things that he shouldn't know about and use that inside information to threaten, scare and intimidate me even more than during our marriage. Domestic abuse during divorce? He was now more inspired than ever to torture me in any and every possible way he could.

He would gloat, showboat, and strut around town mocking me as I would show up confused, disheveled and looking like a frantic mess trying to understand how he always got there first. He would actually stand outside of buildings and say "Yep, here she comes. I knew she would be here," like he had some type of crystal ball that no one else in the world could see. He was acting God-like, and I was feeling confused and intimidated as he laughed at me in front of his large team of bullies he hired to further scare and intimidate me.

I remember a time when a silver pickup truck seemed to be around me for the better part of the day. It's not something you would normally notice, but we lived on a very quiet street, and I saw this truck behind me each time I came home that day. I knew that no one on my street owned a silver pickup truck, so when I parked in my garage I went over to the window and saw it leaving after the third time it had followed me home. Now I realized I was being followed. That night I dropped my son off at a birthday party and sure enough I noticed the silver pickup truck behind me in my rearview mirror. I was furious. I knew the streets well in this neighborhood, so I purposely went down one that was a dead-end with a very narrow spot to turn around at the end. The truck followed me all the way to the bottom. I couldn't believe it. Here we were, a pitch-black night, at the end of the road, and I start thinking, maybe he has been hired not just to follow me, but to kill me. Here I was, at the bottom of a dead-end street, with no room to easily turn around. What had I done?

I am terrified. I'm trapped and there's nothing I can do but turn around, so I drive to the end and start doing so. He does the same. At any moment, as I end up in the other direction and he is doing his turn, we are going to come face-to-face through our windows. I am shaking in my seat. Is he going to pull out a camera? A gun? Will he try and hide his face or stare me down and scare me? I don't think I've ever been so terrified in my life. What started out as a moment of bravery on my part, a moment to stand up for myself against the minion of a man who seemed to be trying to continuously put me down, could have seriously put me in danger, and for what? What was my purpose right now?

As my car is now facing forward I realize I can hit the gas and accelerate quickly, and if he is still facing the end of the road and needs to turn around, he will be delayed before he can come after me. This helps me calm a bit as our windows now get closer and closer to directly lining up. I can't make the moment stop. I can't make our wheels stop turning. And suddenly there we are, face-to-face and stuck in a moment in time that I will never forget. I stare straight into his eyes.

He is a middle-aged man who did not shave that day and has glints of silver stubble in his beard. He's wearing a red baseball cap, and underneath are dark, penetrating eyes staring straight at me. I do not look away, won't look down, just stare right back at him trying to comprehend what is happening, trying to take all of this in. A few moments ago, I was a mom dropping her son off at a birthday party. Now I am a woman, alone on a dark, dead-end street, wondering if I will ever see the light of day again.

So much is whirling through my mind at once that I can barely process my thoughts: *see who he is, see what he wants, did you imagine this whole thing, is this really happening right now or is this just a car making a U-turn behind you*? But I see his face, I see his expression and I know what I need to know. He is there for me. He is clearly terrorizing me and coming within inches of my car without having a single thought about doing so. He stares at me with soulless eyes and a look of malice on his face. I am simply a moving target to him, and I just engaged him in a game. I am nothing but his mark for the night. He is nothing but a hired hand who will get paid to report on where I was and what I did tonight. He takes a final glance at me, smirks, moves his car around mine, and speeds off into the night. But he will leave a fear inside of me that will last for years and a habit of looking in my rearview mirror that remains to this day. The man with the soulless eyes that I never saw again after that night because I could identify his face and his truck. The next day the silver truck was replaced by a blue sedan.

There was such a mob mentality to what they did to me. And none of these large men seemed to notice or care that they were bullying an innocent female who was desperately trying to walk through the days of her life and simply complete the act of being a person and a mom. I say, "shame on you" to all of them, but the rest I leave to God and to Karma. For each can be a real force to be reckoned with when you mess with them, and I wouldn't want to be any of those big scary bullies out there in the world after what they have done to me and countless others. I truly believe, in my heart of hearts, that in the end we all get what we deserve and it is not up to me or any other human to exact revenge on one another. I leave it to God. And that is how I now live a life with as much peace and as much purpose as I can possibly muster.

I take a deep breath before I publish this blog. I am allowing myself to feel a great deal of fear again, and I am bringing it back to make a point, but that doesn't make it any easier on a day like today. Because on a day like today, where I have stopped and allowed myself to feel this fear again, it forces me to remember what I have been through and what it felt like.

Abusers are scary from the day they show us who they truly are, and days and years after that as the truth continues to unfold. They scare us with their words, their body language, and their threats. Fear and intimidation tactics are real if you feel scared. Don't let anyone tell you that it's in your head because that's gaslighting. If you see it, it's real. If you feel it it's real. You and only you decide.

Abusers start off small and then keep upgrading their arsenals until they are carrying things so large we are scared to stillness. Some may even use weapons as well: guns, knives, hidden cameras, tracking devices, Private Investigators, their friends. Anything and anyone can become a weapon if it is used against you to scare you. And they are masterful at this. I don't know if it is learned behavior or they are born with it, but their skill and their expertise at what they do is so impressive that alone we, in the end, will never beat them. We have one and only one choice: to get away before it's too late. Reach out to the professionals to help you.

9

Actions Speak Really Loudly

(WARNING SIGN OF DOMESTIC ABUSE:
Destroys your property or threatens to hurt or
kill your pets)

It's something that every victim of domestic abuse needs to be warned about: how quickly things will escalate once you tell them that you are no longer under their control. You spend a lot of time with your abuser and you think you know them, and the limits of their viciousness, pretty well. But you know them as your abuser, not the person who has just lost control of the one he loves to abuse. You quickly learn that they will stop at nothing when they feel that they have nothing left to lose. They are vested in you, in all the time that they have spent making you feel worthless, and you quickly learn just how damn important you have become to them when you try to quietly slip out of their lives, and how they don't look where they step as they will step on anything to keep getting to you.

The red flags were so bright that they should have burned my eyes and sent me running for the door. But I kept walking towards danger because I was in this pure state of bliss and excitement. I had done it! I was getting out of prison and all I could see was my freedom stretching out in front of me. I did not see the path I had to walk from here to there, I only saw the finish line and missed the mine field that lay between.

I see her coming home from the beach and I want to scream, "Don't do it! Don't go in there!" It's like when you go to see a horror movie and you know that innocent person is walking into a trap, going into the wrong room, heading in the wrong direction. I see her pulling into the driveway and my heart goes out to her. She's not stupid, she's just never been here before. She's been in this garage hundreds of times, but never in this garage on this day in this moment. She's never been here before. She has no idea how much things have changed while she was gone. She has no idea that in cases of domestic abuse, more than 75 percent of abusers turn to violence when the victim tries to leave. Now she is coming back and will try to leave again? What did she just do to her odds? I cringe.

She didn't have a plan because she didn't know that she needed one. She thought that saying she wanted a divorce and finally declaring her independence meant that she would be free. She thought that he would just let her go without a fight. She thought, that like other couples who got a divorce, he would be a man and move out and leave her and the children in their home. But when, in twenty years, had he ever done anything without a fight? It's incredible to think that after all of that abuse that somehow, she thought that he would suddenly change and treat her as real men treated their wives when they wanted to leave. She couldn't explain her thought process; it makes no sense even to this day. It's just that when you are that close to a life that is so bad, when you are sensing your freedom, when you are about to make a break for it, maybe, just maybe you believe that everything will finally be ok. Something in her felt like if she shouted out that she was a victim of abuse, if she finally admitted what she could not admit to herself or others for so many years, if she stood up and told people what was happening, that the abuse would magically stop as the world became her witness. And through those incredible rose-colored glasses you most definitely do not see red danger signals flashing all around you.

I see her pull into the garage, and I'm so sorry for her. She is coming home to a different place. A place far scarier than ever before. She has been gone for a week. A week where he was supposed to cool down, but instead it was a week where he went absolutely crazy and began to put his plan into place. He went through her home office and destroyed all evidence of her large corporate job. He destroyed pay stubs, tax returns, and photo albums of her with celebrities at work parties and celebrations. These files she would desperately need later during her divorce to prove who she was and what she had accomplished and he knew this, so he destroyed them.

He spent the week planting the cameras and microphones in the house. He knew when she returned that she would have a divorce attorney and would make and take calls from their home. He put cameras and microphones in every room that she frequented in the house, all the way down to her dressing room within her closet, so he wouldn't miss a single word she said to anyone.

He placed a tap on her cell phone. Not hard to do since they still share one cell phone account. He now has a record of every single call she makes and at what time and at what frequency. He knows when she hires attorneys, investigators, accountants, anyone that she is talking with. He knows who she is calling for advice and will later subpoena and depose these same people to make them speak under oath about these private conversations.

And he sneaks out in the garage while she is sleeping and places a tracking device on her car. He can now track her every move, know where she is at all times, and know where she is going before she even gets there.

While she has given him a week to cool down, war has been declared within her home, and she has no clue. Why she didn't suspect it just goes to her kind and gentle nature, her naiveté, and to her underestimation of the cruelty of her opponent. She doesn't know yet, but she is coming home and walking into the trap of her life.

He meets her at the door and greets her with a smile. She sees this as a sign of peace and relaxes a bit. She brings her mom and children back into the home. It would be at this point in the movie that watchers would be yelling out, "Don't go in there!" and rightfully so, but she is clueless and just strolls in as he welcomes her back.

He asks her if she wants to change her mind and she says no; she is firm with her decision. She has had months, and now a week of solitude without him breathing down her neck all the time, to really think about this final decision. At what point did he start regarding her as less than a person? At what point did it become ok to treat her like a diseased and contagious human being? She remembers when she fell down the stairs and broke her arm into three pieces. The pain was excruciating, the healing time long. She had reached out to some of her closest friends via email to let them know and to say that she may need some help with carpools or to cover a PTA meeting for her here and there until she was mobile.

As word spread through the community of her accident many people, she found out later, would ask him if she was ok and how they could help. And later she learned that he had told each and every one of them, "She's fine! She's making a big deal out of a little fracture. She's just being a baby." But it was more than a fracture. It was a bone in three pieces, she also had a fracture in her foot, and she was ordered to bed rest. Those that she had reached out to became both confused and worried. Confused because they were hearing two different things, and worried because he told them not to come see her.

The community was starting to see how he regarded her, and they began to take note. Their secret was slowly leaking out, but she didn't know yet because this time he had her in the ultimate state of isolation: bed rest per the doctor, and no visitors because he said so. His dream come true. Her worst nightmare realized.

And what really and truly broke her heart during this time was that their children were beginning to notice how he treated her. One night during this time her son asked her, "Mommy, if Daddy is always angry at you, then why do you stay here?" It was a moment that made her stop talking and catch her breath. She'll never forget it. They were curled up in his bed together reading his bedtime story when his dad came into the doorway and barked at her for doing something wrong. Her child saw the look of sadness cross her face before she regained her composure, smiled at him, and began to read again. Her child saw it. And if he saw it, then his brother saw it. And if they saw it and thought that this was what love was supposed to look like, what marriage was supposed to look like, how husbands were supposed to treat wives, how dads were supposed to treat moms, then what in the world was she teaching them by continuing to live this way right in front of them? They saw it. That's all she needed to know. She had stayed for so many years so they could be a family. Now she had to leave so they could learn what a family looked like and what a family did not look like. It was the final straw. She was out.

"Yes, I am sure, I want a divorce," she says to him, and she sees the darkness pass over his face. She takes the boys upstairs to unpack their bags and get away from him as quickly as possible. Her mom, standing in the kitchen not sure what to do, begins to unpack their food bag. He slowly walks up to her mom and says quietly in her ear, "Don't worry. I will never hurt your daughter." The words hang in the air between them as her mom stares at him, trying to make sense of what he has just said. Who asked him if he was planning on hurting her daughter? What was running through his mind that would cause him to say this? These are the beginning of the larger warning signs that they all missed.

———————

Thinking back on this time makes my pulse race and my heart overflow with sadness. I hate this time in my life more than many others because it was a time, for the first time in so many years, that I had hope, and because I thought that hope was enough. But hope is no substitute for a plan. I look back now and I can only say that I forgive me. I didn't know about the statistics. I didn't know that there was so much help available to me. I didn't know that the man who had scared me with his words, threatened me with his body language, kept me in rooms against my will, controlled my every move and action for two decades, would snap the way he did in one final and desperate attempt to keep me where he wanted me. I didn't know he would turn to acts of violence. I didn't know. The sadness is overwhelming, even to this day, four years later, the sadness is overwhelming.

And it takes every bit of strength and courage that I have left in my body and left in my soul to warn you that I did not know what he would do to my dog and what could possibly happen to you one day, too. Because once hope is lost on the other side, hope that a victim will remain a powerless victim, all bets are off there, too. The stakes are raised and the speed at which events occur happen twice as fast. No one is calm and rational. No one takes the time to think things through. The victim is about to get away and the abuser will stop at nothing, NOTHING, to prevent this from happening. It's so desperately important to me that you please understand this. My dog and I both were unnecessary victims to a man who had already done far too much damage in this world. My loving and bright beacon of hope, my sweet little creature who had come into my life to save me from the sadness of losing my father, who had stood by my side day and night for fifteen years, would first turn into a hostage and then turn into collateral damage. I just didn't know. And the details of that are so horrific that there is no amount of therapy nor help out there for me that will ever make that ok. I can't write about it, I can't talk about it, I can only say, "God help me" when I am forced to think about it. I can't beat myself up because I have suffered far too much already and, unlike him, I did not have cameras, microphones, tracking devices and cellphone taps to tip me off as to what was about to happen. It is a subject that is off limits and even my therapist understands that to go back and discuss this would do far too much damage and not do anything to help, so he calls it a "non-discussion point." It is a story that I have promised myself I will never tell again after being forced to tell and retell during depositions and in public during our last court hearing.

I'll remember that day for the rest of my life. The air got heavy and seemed to cling to itself as I slowly spoke out each word and watched them sink into the ears, minds, souls, of those who were forced to listen to it. I watched five men go still and watch me as I told every explicit detail of this horrific day in my life: three lawyers who had been in courtrooms for over thirty years apiece, a judge who was seasoned and had heard many stories of horror I'm sure, and my ex-husband who sat there and looked me directly in the eye as I held my head up and promised myself that I would not cry in order to make sure that everyone else would understand every word as I spoke it. When I was done I looked up to see that my story had melted the stoic legal masks right off the faces of the three trial attorneys: one stood with his mouth agape, one stood with his eyes locked on me and his face turned ashen white, and the third looked down when our eyes met, but not fast enough that I didn't notice that his eyes were completely filled with tears. The courtroom went silent and our judge, who always spoke in a loud and resounding voice, said in a gentle whisper, that we all had to strain to hear, that we would break for lunch and that we would continue with a new witness when we returned. He too, knew that I had suffered enough.

I stood up and the tears that I had been holding back streamed down my face like a dam had broken. My attorney rushed over to the witness stand and took me by the elbow and guided me out of the courtroom as if I was blind, and in that moment, I was. I didn't see the courtroom any longer. I didn't see my ex-husband. I only saw my beautiful white dog and what had happened to him.

I saw every detail as if it were happening in that courtroom, right in front of me, all over again. I remember going to the cafeteria in the courthouse and my legal team and I sat together at a table. No one spoke, no one ate. An hour later we returned to our hearing without having said a word.

How excruciating and how important it becomes for me to write this next blog for us. It's time to separate the one domestic abuse victim from the other three who are not. It's time to call out who you are, who I am, and who the others are. Do you feel so alone right now? I did for twenty years. The next time you go out do this: count off four people in line at the coffee shop, or at the grocery store, or look around a restaurant at a table of four. Statistics will tell you that one of those four people knows exactly how you feel because this is their life too. If you are not a victim, play the same game, count out four people in line, look at a table for four, look at a doubles tennis match, one of them is most likely a victim. What are you willing to do to help them? Do you have any idea how scared and alone they feel right now?

This blog I write with intention and full-on clarity. If you don't get me by now, then you need to get me right now. There is a huge difference between a marriage, a bad marriage, and a marriage of domestic abuse. I have seen all three in my life, in different ways and at different times. But I know all three when I see them, and I want you to know them, too. Make no mistake about it, they are nothing alike and I'm making it our job to understand the differences so we can get in there and do something about it.

Marriage: The Good, the Bad, and the Ugly

I think most of us remember that all-too-famous movie line, "You complete me." We waited to hear it the whole time we watched, and when we did, at least for me, we felt joy and happiness and relief that this beautiful couple would come back together. I mean, they completed one another, right?

I often hear people say that marriage is 50/50. I want to scream, "No it's not! Marriage is 100/100!" This is a critical concept for all of us to understand, especially those who are victims of domestic abuse. There are critical differences between a good marriage, a bad marriage, and a marriage of domestic abuse. As SODAs™ we often miss the signs. I'm not sure why, but we do.

Marriage: The Good. I grew up in a home where a really good marriage was modeled by my parents. They were so in love! I was truly blessed. Did my parents argue sometimes? Of course they did. Did they pick on one another sometimes? Of course they did. What did a good marriage look like? They were in love, they were always kind, and they apologized if one of them said something that hurt the other one's feelings. There were no threats, there was nothing scary in that home. There was a marriage built on love, mutual respect, give and take, and showing up and giving 100% all the time.

Marriage: The Bad. I have seen these marriages too. Sadly, I have seen too many. These are the marriages where two really good people are just not in love anymore. They are trying to keep it together, for the sake of once having been in love, or the children, or just not wanting to get a divorce. But the truth is that they are no longer in love. They fight all the time. They may sleep in separate bedrooms, they really don't want to do anything together, and they are just miserable all the time. There are no threats, there is nothing scary going on, and in fact there is just a lot of sadness in the home. They are headed for divorce, and it will hurt. But no one will be injured as a result.

Marriage: The Ugly. This one I am way too familiar with. This is the marriage of domestic abuse. And rather than say anything more about it, it is just a great place to list the 15 warning signs that you are living with domestic abuse. There is no better way to address this:

1. Tells you that you can never do anything right.
2. Shows extreme jealousy of your friends and time spent away
3. Keeps you or discourages you from seeing friends or family members
4. Insults, demeans, or shames you with put-downs
5. Controls every penny spent in the household
6. Takes your money or refuses to give you money for necessary expenses
7. Looks at you or acts in ways that scare you
8. Controls who you see, where you go, or what you do
9. Prevents you from making your own decisions
10. Tells you that you are a bad parent or threatens to harm or take away your children
11. Prevents you from working or attending school
12. Destroys your property or threatens to hurt or kill your pets
13. Intimidates you with guns, knives or other weapons
14. Pressures you to have sex when you don't want to or do things sexually you're not comfortable with
15. Pressures you to use drugs or alcohol

There is a message here and it is HUGE. It's urgent for us SODAs™ and truly everyone to get this. Relationships and marriages are amazing when they are give and take. Some days you may give more, some days you may take more and that is fine IF you are fine. 100/100 doesn't mean that each person does everything and doesn't support or help the other. It means that each person comes to the table 100% complete and ready to support the other and also ready to ask for what they need. 100% ready to give and 100% ready to receive. The only way to learn how to do that in a healthy way is to first learn how to do it on your own. So often, victims of domestic abuse run to another man to help them get out. But they haven't healed from their own abuse yet, haven't learned how to be complete, and they accidentally walk right into another cycle of abuse. Please don't do that. There are free resources across the US just for this reason. Please use them.

If you are living a life of domestic abuse you have the choice every single day to end the cycle. If you don't recognize yourself in the mirror any longer, if you are someone that you didn't used to be, if you feel weak, or scared, or afraid of your partner, then something is wrong. If you are forced to do things that you don't want to do, if you have no control over your daily life, if he is destroying your property, or threatening to hurt or kill your pets, then you need to ask yourself why you are willing to keep living like this. And, most importantly, you DO NOT have to find a new partner to help you get out! You simply need to seek the free and professional help that is available to you 24 hours a day and 7 days a week. Make that call, make that plan with them, and start your path to safety, and ultimately to the beginning of your own completion.

Remember this: STRENGTH + SUPPORT + PLAN = FREEDOM. You can do this.

_____

Of course, we know that I came from a marriage of "The Ugly." That's what we have when we are victims of domestic abuse. We don't have good marriages; we don't have bad marriages that used to be good but have just run out of steam; we have ugly, dysfunctional, and toxic marriages that in the end could destroy us if we don't get out of them. So why did I finally break and leave? Why after twenty years was enough finally enough? For sure it was the realization that my children were seeing our marriage and thinking that this is what love looked like. For sure it was that my children were seeing their mom treated like a piece of garbage and thinking that this is how a man treated a woman. For sure it was to show my boys that women are strong enough to get out of these situations and begin again, to create new lives, to make new beginnings and to do it with grace, and that we are more than capable of doing this on our own.

But I also did it for me. It was the last call of my survival instinct and I had just enough strength to answer it. My health was failing. I was getting sicker and sicker by the day: high blood pressure, low blood sugar, weight gain, hair failing out, thyroid dysfunction, it was all coming at me. Coupled with anxiety, depression, and crippling panic attacks. The last call that my survival instinct ever placed was simple: *get out before you die. One way or the other, by his hand or by your own ambivalence, you will die if you stay here with him.*

And the painful, slow death of the eternal optimist was also at play. You know all about this right? We simply believe for far too many years that we will somehow be ok, that this isn't as bad as it really is, that we're just tired or worn out and probably overreacting because they tell us that we are. I had believed that we were a we! I now knew differently. We had never been a team, we had never been a partnership, *we* had never been. I now knew that he would never change. I now knew who I was dealing with at all times. I saw his cruelty grow through the years, I saw his intimidation tactics grow through the years. And I saw something new that was so horrifying to me that I could not ignore it. I saw him enjoying my demise. He mocked my weight gain, he taunted me for being "sick all the time," and he watched me having panic attacks the way someone would make popcorn and watch their favorite movie. He was so enjoying watching me die a slow death that I was now sure he wouldn't mind watching me die a quick one either. I finally woke up and saw my life for what it was: the life of a victim of serious domestic abuse.

As we begin to approach the end, I hope and I pray that I have gotten my messages across. I hope that I have said enough times to make a plan with professionals before you leave. I hope that I have explained that those professionals are your source of strength and that you really do not need anyone else if you have them help you do this. I hope that I have made it clear that running to a new partner while trying to leave the current one is almost always disastrous because if you don't heal yourself first you are not going to be able to build a new and healthy relationship with someone else.

And if you don't learn why you got trapped and how you got trapped then don't you stand a huge chance of just walking in a new place and getting trapped? The best thing you can do is to repair the relationship with yourself and your family, friends, children, and community until you feel so solid on your own feet that you know you can handle whatever life throws at you, and if you don't like what life is throwing, you'll duck and walk away. Please help you first.

I feel a new knot form in my stomach as I publish this blog. Not because it was hard to write, in fact, it was by far one of the easiest. I sit here as still and quiet as the night because I know what I need to do next and it is going to take every last bit of strength that I have left to get through this.

I need to write the final chapter and I need to write the final blog. I need to tell you what happened that night and how it changed my life forever, why it motivated me to write this book, and how I am desperately trying to keep it from happening to you. I take a deep breath but my hands won't stop shaking. It's not just the fear. It's the release of so much pain and so many repressed emotions that have been trying to come out for so many years, but I just wasn't ready to let them. I don't know why now, and I'm not sure how I've done this, but I started the journey, I walked the path, and I see the end right in front of me. There is no going back now. We're in this together. We have to cross this finish line, so let's go do that.

10
Don't Shake the Can

We met when I was 21. I left when I was 41. I remember lying in bed one night before I left and doing the math. If I stayed with this man one more day, which would lead to one more day, which I then knew would become another year, he would have changed half of my life. That thought felt like poison running through my veins.

The first half of my life was amazing. It was everything I wanted it to be and more. A living dream.

He had come into the second half.

In the beginning, it felt like the dreams were continuing. The man of my dreams, the job of my dreams, the home of my dreams, all happening at the same time. But slowly I realized I had entered a nightmare in which I was now trapped with him. And somehow, I stayed there for twenty years. A long and torturous twenty years sprinkled only with the sparkling hope – hope generated by my children, my family, and my friends who showed me that dreams could still be real if I could wake myself up and stop sleep-walking through my life.

And so, something snapped in me that one night. Something spoke to me. Something said: *If you stay here any longer, he defines half of your life. Your amazing life that you have everything to be thankful for will now be defined as half a life of abuse. What are you still doing here?*

Does it make it any better that my life is defined as twenty years of abuse and not half? Somehow it does to me. Somehow in that moment I decided that I had to start taking my power back and stop letting someone else decide what the definition of my life would be. I was the writer, words were mine again, and I would write the title for my own life. So I did. I just did it completely wrong.

———————

I see her at age twenty-one. She is young and so beautiful. She is also quite shy and demure. He, in turn, is much more experienced, confident, and thirty-five years old. She tells him that she wants to take things slowly so she can get to know him. He laughs at her and calls her a little child.

On their second date, he tells her that he is ready to experience her. But she is not ready! She tries to stall him and ask for more time but he won't hear of it. "Women my age don't leave men waiting," he tells her with a sneer, "Why would you make me wait? That's ridiculous." Not wanting to lose him she gives in.

It's just another piece of herself that she will give away to him never to receive back. One piece in a lifetime of compromises, an unrelenting will to please, which ultimately will be her undoing.

Every time she says yes but wants to say no she is giving away more of her power, saying goodbye to who she used to be, but she has no idea in that moment what she is doing to herself.

I often tell the story of the salt water and the brick because it fits so perfectly to my life story. I was a powerhouse my whole life: a brick so to speak. Then I met my husband, angry, bitter, spewing insults at me: the salt water. And what does salt water do to a brick? You wouldn't think much right? Because bricks are so strong. But bricks made in the 60s, 70s, and 80s were not made to be salt tolerant, and I, being a product of the 1970s, fit into this story perfectly.

Brick homes placed by the sea were hit each day with a spray of salt water and guess what happened? Hit repeatedly by the salty spray, they slowly started to crumble and disintegrate. Was it visible at first? Nope. Did anyone know? Not early on. And the oddest part? The salt crystals got inside, expanded, broke the brick down, and the structures crumbled from the inside before they collapsed. Wow. It sounds so much like my life story. I was the brick. He was the salt water, each day hurling a spray of acrid insults, fear, intimidation, control, and isolation over me that, as it sank in, changed who I was, and eventually I crumbled from the inside out.

Why do I point out that these bricks that failed were from the 1960s, 70s, and 80s? Because people have since corrected these bricks and made new and stronger bricks that will withstand salt water. But have we? What have we done with our daughters, sisters, friends, and mothers to make them newer and stronger than before? Who is warning them about the salt water that is out there? Salt water that will look and feel so refreshing at first and then crumble you from the inside out? What do we need to do? One of three things: make stronger bricks, don't leave homes unattended by the sea, or pick up the homes that are stuck there and move them away. It's one of these three choices and we need to get it done. It's exactly the same with victims of domestic abuse.

I see him as he weakened her over the years. I see him penetrating into her soul, into her being, into her largest crevices to implant himself and then expand so that eventually she would crumble. I see him removing love to hurt her. I see him refusing to ever hold her hand or give her a hug or put his arm around her. I see him withholding sex to starve her and make her feel alone and not connected to anyone in the world. I see him kissing her on the altar at their wedding and never again kissing her on the lips. Not for twenty years. Never again. These were all ways that he weakened her from the inside out. She is a warm, loving and affectionate woman. He took that away from her, slowly crumbling her along the way.

They were not into drugs and they didn't drink much. She was afraid to drink around him because she needed to always be fully aware of him and what he would do. She couldn't allow herself to relax for fear of her safety. He would have an occasional beer, but it just didn't mean much to either of them. His drug of choice? Her.

He got addicted to the pleasure of torturing her. He had unlimited access to her, and punishing her became his high. And like most drug users, after a while he needed more and more to get where he wanted to be. He would scare her, get the reaction he needed, and each day the adrenaline would wear off sooner than the day before. So, what next? He would come back for more as quickly as possible. Whatever went wrong in his day became her fault. Whatever scared him in life, whatever frustrated him, whatever got on his nerves, whenever he was bored, she was his drug, his toy, his everything, and he couldn't get enough.

The irony was overwhelming. He took a great deal of her power in the beginning by convincing her to share her body before she was ready. Her body. The most personal thing in the world to her. And, in the end, he did the same thing again. He took away her power by doing the one thing that she never thought he would do; he injured her body. Her body. The most personal thing in the world to her. That same arm that had been broken into three pieces when she fell down the stairs. That same woman who had laid still in terror begging for help at the bottom of the staircase. He lost control and went in for the kill, and her arm ended up damaged and dangling by her side all over again. And she never saw it coming.

I see her declare that she is leaving. She was removing his drug right from his addicted hands; she really shook the hell out of his soda can in that final effort to set herself free. He reacted the same way any addict would. He went into a blind rage. No one takes drugs away from an addict, least of all this silly little girl. She was going to pay for it. And she did.

She'll never forget that day and she'll never forget that night. It would become the subject of countless recalls. So many "what happened?" moments. So many times she would retell the story to police, detectives, judges, lawyers, on the stands in courtrooms, in conference rooms during depositions, to friends, to family, and later to male friends who walked up too quickly on her and startled her and then jumped after she screamed in fright. The night that will not die. The night she would not die. The night that will never go away. The night she finally got away. The night she barely got away.

It must have become real, too real, for him when he found out that she was looking to rent a home, a very large and lovely home, about three miles from where they lived. She finally realized that he would not move out of their home, that he would fight to the death for it, and after knowing that the house had been full of cameras and microphones and so much ugliness and contamination, she decided that she no longer wanted to live there.

Her day had started out walking through the rental home with her mom and the real estate agents. It was amazing! She loved everything about it, had friends living on the same street and loved the neighborhood. The house had large grounds, a swimming pool, and everything that her boys would be looking for in a second home, so she signed the rental agreement on the spot. This place was perfect!

The homeowner gave her the keys and told her she could move in that day. She couldn't believe her good fortune. Things were looking up and she was making her clean start! All she had to do was get to her old home and meet her boys at the bus stop, and then she would bring them over to show them the place and they could have a pizza party and sleepover that same night. She was bubbling over with excitement when her cell phone rang.

"Hello?" she answered as she saw the boys' school phone number on her Caller ID.

"Um, Susan?" the School Secretary asked rather nervously.

"Yes?" she answered, suddenly full of dread.

"Um, we have it in our notes that the boys go home with you today."

"Yes," she answered, "That's right. I'll meet them at the bus stop."

"Well, um, we tried to stop him but...uh...you should probably get up here right now..."

"WHAT?" she started to breathe hard into the phone, "Stop ... what?"

"Well, he showed up and insisted that he was taking the boys early from school today and we could not stop him. He took your older son. Since you are not divorced we do not have a Custody Order in place, only your notes on the temporary schedule. I'm so sorry but we had to let him go..."

"Oh my God...ok...I'll be right there..."

And I see her, dressed so beautifully in a designer dress and high heels and a knit poncho with fringe trim, in her new rental home, running as fast as she can to her car, jumping in, screaming to her mom to grab her purse, and off they race to the elementary school to try and figure out what just happened.

––––––––––––

The events of this day began at 1:50 p.m. and ended at 1:50 a.m. By the time I got home from the hospital it was almost 4 a.m., but by then it was all over and behind me. I was in shock, and I barely remember being walked to the safety of the sofa at my mom's home and placed gingerly down with the help of my brother and sister-in-law. I had one working arm and one arm wrapped and strapped to my body in a sling. Fire burned down my side every time I forgot and tried to use my shoulder or my arm.

I lay there from 4 a.m. until 7:30 a.m. the next morning staring at the ceiling, thinking over and over again about what had happened. Then I got up and went to the Family Justice Center where everyone was waiting for me. It was time to stand up for myself, get a restraining order, and put some protection between myself and my husband.

But, as you can see, it was too late. The damage was done. I was already injured. The details are so painful to recall, the moments so hard to discuss. I gently fill in the blanks only to tell you, once and again, have a plan, don't go in alone, don't go in at all, please just don't.

But for me, a mom, any mom, what would we do? He had used the ultimate bait and made it impossible not to follow. He had taken my child and I didn't know where he was or what was going to happen. If you have children then you know what I know: there is no worse fear, there is no worse feeling of dread, and you feel it in your stomach like a knot that cannot be untied. As moms, we are only as happy as our saddest child. We are only as healthy as our sickest. Only as strong as our weakest. He had taken my son, and I didn't know where they were.

* * *

WARNING SIGN OF DOMESTIC ABUSE #10:
Threatens to harm or take away your children

The day then turned into a nightmare of police, frantic calls, and her pleading in text messages with him to just bring her son home. But this was all a part of his plan to completely undo her one final time, and he was soaking up the moment and loving every single second of it.

He spent the next several hours taunting her in an unrelenting fashion. "We were just here..." he would text, "...but now we are not." She would never know where they were, only that they were out and about. She knew that her son was ok, but she didn't know how this day was going to end. She kept calling and pleading with the police to help her, but there was nothing that the police could do because they were still married. This was just a dad out with his son, there was nothing unusual going on as far as the law was concerned.

When he finally returned home with her son after more than eight hours he was exuberant, gloating, and absolutely glowing. Her son, having no idea what had been going on, was excited to show her that he had gotten a new bike and had gone out to dinner. He announced that he was "sleeping at dad's tonight" because dad had promised him all the brownies he could eat and no bedtime on a school night!

She was exhausted, exasperated, and relieved to see that their little boy was ok, but she wasn't leaving him behind. Not after that day. She knew this was far from over. In fact, she knew this was only the beginning. She was dizzy with the events of the day and night and knew she wasn't leaving their home; she wasn't even sure that she could safely drive her car. She just needed sleep so badly, so she told her husband that she and her mother and their younger son would sleep there as well that night, and she headed up to her bedroom for one final night of sleep there and a proper goodbye to a home and a room that had once been filled with so many dreams of a bright future.

But he would have nothing of it and he followed her up the stairs so closely that she could feel his hot breath on her neck. "You don't live here anymore!" he screamed at her as she walked into the bedroom, "Get out of here!"

"Please," she pleaded quietly with him, "This has been a terrible day for all of us, just please leave this room and let me go to sleep.

Let the boys have the sleepover you promised them and I will pack the rest of my things and be out of here first thing in the morning."

The events of the day, coupled with his rage over knowing that she had signed the lease on her new home, were too much for him to bear. He stormed over to the bed, the bed that they had shared for almost twenty years, and started throwing everything on the floor. He threw the pillows, the comforter, and started tearing off the sheets.

"What are you doing?" she asked in confusion as fear started to climb up her body from her toes to the base of her spine, "Why are you doing that?"

"You are not sleeping in this room, you will not touch these sheets, you will leave this home and you will leave the children with me!" he yells at her, "Get out of this house! Get out of here!"

She is so terrified by his tone that she pauses and does not move. She doesn't think she's ever seen him this angry. She knows that she cannot leave without the boys. She senses with every fiber of her being that they are in danger, and she will not leave them behind. She does not want them to substitute for her, to have to bear the brunt of his anger, an anger she sees as growing rage. She senses that she is not safe either, but she can't see a choice in that moment. Her mom is in this home, his parents are in this home, their children are in this home, yet she sees a rage and a loss of focus in his eyes that tells her that he only sees her: this moment, and their final destiny on the last page of their book together as a married couple, in this room, on this night. She can see that nothing else matters. His butterfly has sprung loose from his web and he is in a state of rage and disbelief that has detached him from reality.

She sits on the edge of the bed to catch her breath and to think about what she is going to do. He sits down on the opposite side of the bed across from her and stares at her with fury, "I am telling you one final time to get off of this bed, out of this room, and out of this house right now," and he finishes what he has begun, continuing to rip the blankets, sheets, and remaining bedding off the bed, pulling everything out from under her body making her lose her balance. She grabs a corner of the comforter to steady herself as she starts to tip over in his direction and he sees that she is now within his reach. He lunges toward her, grabs her by the wrist and pulls quickly as he tries to throw her on the floor on his side of the bed with the bedding that is already down there.

His movements are so swift and powerful that she feels her body take flight as he pulls her towards him. She sees the bed underneath her and watches her body go soaring directly towards his. Life stands still in that single moment. Such an odd feeling to lose control of your own body. It was the same feeling when she fell down the staircase. She had no control. She is a weightless, lifeless, ragdoll to his superhuman strength. She feels nothing, she sees nothing, she just watches her body fly through space. She is heading directly towards his lap and trying to scramble not to land on him. She has never been more terrified in her life. Please God don't let me land on him. He will pin me down, he will hurt me, I am so sure of it.

She doesn't even know at this point that she is already injured, that having her full body weight pulled by her wrist, across a bed, with a force to make her fly, was going to do some serious damage. She has never felt a fear like that in her life, she feels her own heart beating as if it is screaming, and she is afraid that she will stop breathing.

She lands one inch from his knees and scurries back as quickly as possible from his body before he can strike at her again. She pushes herself off the bed backwards and lands on the floor on the other side. She jumps to her feet and starts running as fast as she can. She recognizes that she is running for her life. She has seen his eyes, seen his lack of soul, and she knows what he is thinking.

She screams to her mother to grab the car keys and she screams to the boys that they are getting out. She is screaming at him to leave her alone, he has won, she will leave. Pure fear and adrenaline carry her out of the bedroom as all hell starts to break loose in their home.

———————

When I reflect back I see this night in bits and pieces because to see it as the whole story is too much for me to bear. I see waves of fear, screams, horror, and I remember the searing pain in my arm that he has torn from my shoulder. I see flashing red and blue police lights. I see my children screaming. I see my mom being knocked against the staircase wall. I see terror on everyone's faces. I see people running in all directions, doors being slammed and locked, children hiding in closets. I see them putting me on a stretcher and taking me to the hospital again. I see it.

It happened to me because I went back to an unsafe place. I stood up to my abuser and I didn't have a plan. All of this could have been avoided if I had never set foot back in that home again. He lured me back by baiting me, and I fell for it. He knew exactly what he was doing. I could have been smarter and brought some help, but he was one step ahead of me, and I still simply wasn't looking out for his violence.

More than seventy-five percent of us get injured when we try and leave. I said it before and I will say it as many times as it takes. More than seventy-five percent of us get injured when we try and leave.

The thing about domestic abuse is this: it's based on fear and intimidation and scare tactics that our abusers craft with their words, actions, and body language. So as victims we learn what our lives are going to be like and we somehow make this our "normal"; we learn how to dance within the lines so as not to get hurt. But what we don't count on, in so many instances, is what will happen when our abusers tip over the edge? Why do we think that just because they have always used words and body language that they may not one day pick up a knife, or cock a fist back, or grab us by the arm and throw us across a room? Why do we count on the fact that just because it has not happened yet, it will never happen? I always said, "He'll never touch me, he never has." You know what? That was true until the day it wasn't.

_____

Don't Shake the Can...

Not long ago I stood in front of hundreds of people and made a heartwarming speech. I said, "It takes a village. You thought I was talking about raising my kids, right? No, I was talking about all of the people that it took to get me to this day." To that I heard a lot of laughter which is exactly what I wanted. I expected that they knew what I was talking about. We all shared that moment together and we all shared that laugh. Laughter is so great during times of incredible stress, but in the end, there is nothing funny about domestic abuse.

I looked up in that moment and I saw my village. I saw my family, I saw my children, I saw my neighbors, and I saw my friends. I saw the receptionist from my doctor's office who always worked me in as I got sicker and sicker from stress because she knew what was going on. I saw my friend who helped me get a rental home within 24 hours when I had to flee mine. I saw my best friends who had checked on me daily for four years straight once they had finally been let in on what had been going on. I saw the people who had never left my side because they always knew, even while I didn't know they knew. But here we were, in this one single moment, all knowing, and I felt more love and more strength than I have ever felt in my entire life. I was a bubble floating in air right in front of them. I was becoming whole again, and we were all celebrating this victory together.

During my years of domestic abuse, I can't tell you how many days I sat isolated in my home feeling like I had no friends left. Like if I told anyone what was truly going on they would run away, not wanting to have to deal with the terrible truth of my real life. I can't tell you how many nights I fell asleep crying and feeling like the only person left on the planet. I felt so alone. Even when people were around me I felt alone because no one knew the truth of how horrible my life was. My family had some idea, maybe more than I knew, but truly, no one could see all of the awful reality.

But once I fell down those stairs, and my husband tried to completely isolate me, everything finally began to change. I just couldn't hold it in any longer and I opened up to my family and closest friends about what was going on. It was a slow process where I let a little out and tested for a reaction. I told them how he wasn't talking to me and how I was on bed rest and helpless and how only my mom and children were helping me. They reacted in sadness, disbelief, and horror. They asked me how they could help. They asked me what I needed. They asked me what they could do to get me through this until I was strong enough to do something for myself.

And in those moments, I started to learn something that would forever change my life. Telling people the truth felt GOOD. Letting this out felt GREAT. Knowing that help was available and that I was no longer alone made me feel STRONGER. I was alone in a bedroom with one working arm and I began to feel stronger than I had in twenty years? Ok, something big was happening here.

But I didn't realize at the time that I was doing something really dangerous. I was beginning to shake the can of a really combustible and dangerous situation. While finally telling my friends and family what was going on felt amazing, the people I really needed to be confiding in were the experts who could help me get out safely with a plan. While it felt great to finally let out my secrets and not feel like a victim anymore, it was not so safe to do this not knowing who may or may not turn around and tell my husband what I was saying. And doing so while still living with him and being within the confines of my bedroom and his rule was downright dangerous.

And while it was wonderful to be met with compassion, tissues, tears, and sympathy, none of these wonderful people who were my village were trained to help me get out safely, without injury, without getting killed, and without having anyone else in my family get hurt as well.

I was playing a very unsafe game without knowing it, and this is the cautionary tale that I have been telling all along. Once we start shaking that can, we just want to shake and shake and shake. Because you know what? It feels GOOD. We finally are taking some of our power back, and it's about damn time. But the problem with that is the timing. It's not the right time to start telling your story when you are still inside. When you are still inside it's the time to remain calm, quiet, and make your plan with the professionals to get out safely.

When you are out and on the other side, in a safe place, and at a safe distance, by all means tell your story day and night and night and day. By then you will have been trained by the experts on what the statistics are, what to look for, how to watch your own back, and what to do and what not to do. This is all of the training and information that I missed out on because I didn't know how to get it. And in the end, I paid for it and had to make my great escape with only one working and functional arm – an arm that had healed from a fall down a staircase and had been reinjured on a night that I will never forget. That definitely slowed me down, made everything a whole lot harder, and left me with horrific memories that I will never be able to erase. And the hell of it is that in actuality I was lucky; he could have done so much worse.

You have people available that are trained to help you and ready to go. When you call the professionals, they will tell you exactly how to get started. You can walk into any religious dwelling (a church, a temple, you name it) and ask for the clergy and they will help you. You can search for "family justice center" online and see if one exists in your area. You can search under domestic abuse and you will be shocked to see how many free places exist in your area full of people waiting to help you. You can talk to your doctor. You can drive right up to a police or fire station. All of these people will help you because it is part of their jobs to do so. From there you will build your village.

After you assemble your group of experts you can then ask about free support groups full of other domestic abuse victims, and it is here that you will meet your new friends. Here you will find support like you have never seen because these are the other SODA™ bubbles that have already burst free. They are there waiting for you. They will tell you their stories and listen to yours. They will be there for you because they know what you are going through and what you have been through. It is here that you will move past the sympathy of your family and friends and find the empathy that reminds you that what you have been through is real, and of the strength it took to survive and decide to thrive. YOU ARE NOT ALONE. We are everywhere. One in four women will experience domestic abuse in our lifetimes.

Remember this: STRENGTH + SUPPORT + PLAN = FREEDOM. You can do this.

I see me. It is a dark world out there, or at least it can be. The days can be dark, the nights even darker. He tried to dull my edges that once were sharp and so bright. I was a diamond in the rough, but he didn't polish me and make me more brilliant. He wore me down and made me lose those edges.

As with so many abuse victims who finally escape their marriages, I thought it was over once I got out. Even though I got hurt on the way out, I thought it was finally finished. Little did I know that it was simply the start of a new chapter of my life. I had so much still to endure, and I endure to this day.

Like most abusers, he did not give up or give in easily. He continued to abuse. It took more than five years to struggle to a day where I could start to live with peace in my heart again. And then, and only then, did I begin to think that I had to do something to help the others who would follow behind me, who were still stuck, or who may be about to step into the same trap.

This is an incredibly hard life, one that is hard when you discover what you have gotten stuck with, one that is harder to walk away from, and one that is the most difficult to heal from. There is so much work to be done, and it's an incredible journey that sometimes seems like a never-ending path.

I'm forty-six now. I sit in front of my laptop and I have one thing left to give. I have me. I am still a spark. I am a spark that refuses to go out on a dark day. I am a spark that refuses not to shine on a darker night. I don't shine for me, I shine for you. Because if I can show a path, light the way, flash across a darkened sky, then I still have a purpose here. My life and what I have been through has a purpose that doesn't dull my edges but dulls the edges of the pain that I endured for over two decades.

I see me. As I am now. Tempered by all I have been through. I am a fighter. Not with boxing gloves. Not with weapons. But with words. My words are the tools that I will use to change this world for the better in any way that I can. I fought and I fought to get them back, and I will never let them go again. I had them as long as I can remember, and they belong to me. I am resilient and I know that these words, this voice, after all of this, have to mean something to someone. And I pray that they mean something to you, or your sister, or your daughter, or your next-door neighbor, or your mother, or your friend when the group of you go out to lunch and statistics show that one of you is a victim of domestic abuse. Which one of you is it?

I can't go back and change what happened to me. I can't go back and change what has happened to you. But maybe we can stop what could happen to someone else. And maybe we can stop what is still happening to many.

I claim my new life with energy and enthusiasm. Every day I work on who I am and who I still want and need to be. He changed me in many ways, and it is my job to see what I can do about that. But there is one thing that he cannot do and will never be able to do; he can throw all the salt water that he wants, he will never be able to put out my spark. He will never corrode who I am. At my core, I am strong.

I put my hand on the "SEND" button and smile in joy and pain and relief. We did it. We just crossed the finish line together. Are we done? No. Did we just do something together? I really hope so. I will spend the next days, months, and years, praying every single night that we just did something together that will change the world. One in four. I want to see that change in my lifetime. I want to see you make a plan. I want to see you leave safely. I want to see that number change. I want you to all live happy and safe lives. I want the best for you, I want everything for you that I did not have for twenty years. I am here cheering you on. Please be safe, please be happy, and please get help. And please remember the most important part of this entire journey: You are not alone.

Sparks in Love: Epilogue

We live in the same town, I see him all the time. The man who ruined my days, terrified me at night, and took two decades of my life still haunts my dreams and turns them to nightmares even to this day. I attend trauma therapy twice a week and rebuild my life sometimes day by day, sometimes hour by hour, and still even sometimes minute by minute. But it's a credit to me and to all those around me that I've made it to this day. Because I thrive, I love, and I carry on the life that I now live. The life I leave behind is dark, but a spark lives within me and I know that I'm here for a reason, I'm here for a purpose, and I'm meant to do something so much bigger than even I might understand.

I sit here on a sunny day and look at the lovely room I am in. It's my new home. I sit in my home office and watch the sun stream through the window and light up the lovely shades of copper and green fabric wallpaper as I contemplate the incredible path that I have traversed.

It was twenty years of terror, sprinkled with moments of joy, which ended with a night that still terrifies me when I think back on it. But it really didn't end there. In fact, it was just the beginning in so many ways. Getting out was the end of the marriage. Surviving and getting to this day was the beginning of the next chapter. I think about how I could fill book after book with what I have been through since I left: police at my home day and night; tracking devices on my car again; more private detectives following me; intense harassment from my husband as we went through separation, court battles, the divorce, custody trials; and moving from home to home trying to find a place where I could feel safe again. Oh, what I have been through, oh what I still have to say about it.

But the main focus of this book for me was this: to help, to hope, and to heal. When I was beginning my journey of healing from domestic abuse I searched and searched for books about people who had been through what I had been through so I could find out how they had made it out and if they were now ok. I was looking for a beacon of hope. A person who had been through what I had and would tell me that I would make it through this. I wanted something and someone to hold onto. I needed to find a way to begin the healing process, I needed reassurance, and books had always been a place where I started when looking to make a change in my life.

There was plenty of professional advice available. But I couldn't find the book I was looking for, a book that told the story about the woman who got trapped inside of domestic abuse and lived to tell her story of triumph. I was looking for the one that told me that it was ok that I made that mistake, and that one in four of us do that, and that I was not the damaged goods that I had been told I was. I was looking for the book that told me what all of the warning signs were so I could one day share it with the young women in my own life and warn them, educate them, and use it to help tell my own story as a means of coping, repairing, restoring, and coming back to me.

I was looking for the book that would, just maybe, inspire others to get up and get out if they were stuck, because if I had been stuck for twenty years maybe, they would know that any amount of time is just not too long. It's never too late to get yourself out. It just isn't. Life is such a precious gift, there is no reason to live it trapped inside a terrible life. I wanted someone to tell me that! I needed someone to tell me that.

And I was looking for the book that would tell me that this can happen to anyone. It doesn't happen only to the weak, only to the poor, only to the rich, only to the anything. This happens to one in four women. One in four women out to lunch at a fancy restaurant. One in four women teaching classes at an elementary school. One in four women living in poverty in an inner city. One in four women running for political office. One in four women staying at home raising their children. One in four women working their way up the corporate ladder. One in four. I was looking for the book that would tell me that so that I could feel better that I was the one in four, the book that would validate me and my experiences by telling of the similar experiences of others, but I couldn't find it. I just couldn't find it.

So, what does it mean to be a SODA™? What does it mean to be a Survivor Of Domestic Abuse? We know. Those of us who are "one in four" know. When I tell people about my twenty years of abuse they look at me with sadness and disbelief, sometimes curiosity, and often sympathy. Sometimes I see confusion in their eyes, as in, "You seem so strong, how did this happen to you?" Other times I see admiration in their eyes, as in, "You are so strong, good for you for getting out."

And for me, I see it as both. And for you, maybe you do too. Domestic abuse can happen to anyone. Anyone. And it is not up to any of us to doubt, judge, or over-analyze why when it happens to us – or to others. It's just up to us to help, understand, educate, and throw a lifeline whenever we can to those who are still in there. When I look back at my life I see when I was weak and I see when I was strong. But I often say this and I live my life this way: "It's not how you start but how you end that matters." So, if somehow you have stepped off the path and want to have a happy ending that is still up to you. It doesn't matter how it started, the middle will become a blur one day, and the real question is: what do you want your ending to look like? Because it didn't happen yet: your ending, my ending, the ending. It didn't happen yet. It's all yours for the taking. So, what do you want your ending to look like? To say every ending is a picture-perfect happy ending is naïve. To say every ending can be filled with peaceful days and star-filled nights, that is a reality. I am here on the other side to tell you loud and clear that you can have peace again. You can have a life where you are not afraid, you are not threatened, controlled, demeaned, diminished, embarrassed, and worse. You can have a life where you make your own decisions, choose your own path, and decide who you want to be. It's baby steps. It's one foot in front of the other. But it is possible, and the resources listed in this book are standing by to tell you how to do this because you are not alone. You've never been alone, you probably just feel like you are. I did. I felt alone for twenty years.

I'm not a character in a novel. I'm a human being, just like you. You see me at the grocery store, you see me at the movies with my children, you see me out to dinner. I'm a one in four and I see you, too. You're not hiding in the shadows as much as you think you are. It's not all behind closed doors even though you may be fighting with all you have to keep it there. I see you look at his face before you speak to be sure the words you are choosing not upsetting him. I see you take a small step backwards wh you make that mistake and he starts to get angry in public. I se And the only way I know how to help you is right here, through these pages, where I can reach out and touch you without risking the safety of either one of us. Words were his weapon so I moved away to where I cannot hear them and they cannot reach me. Words are my magic, and I use them every day to spread a message to everyone in the world who needs to hear it: I see you and you are not alone. I am Susan Sparks, survivor of domestic abuse. I now thrive. You, too, can choose to survive. You, too, can choose to thrive. It is my hope that in sharing my story, I have inspired you to make the choice to do so. Thank you for taking this journey with me. It is not a journey that ends today, and it is not a journey that ends until you are safe, they are safe, we all are safe. It is for that reason that I will continue to try to light a path to safety for all who need it.

THE END

more from Susan Sparks and information on statewide and national Domestic Abuse resources, please visit www.TheSoda-Pop.com.

Coming Soon: Sparks in Flight: Saving Susan©
All Rights Reserved 2018

If you are a victim of domestic abuse or domestic violence or want further information PLEASE contact THE NATIONAL DOMESTIC VIOLENCE HOTLINE at: 1-800-799-7233 or TTY 1-800-787-3224. If you are going to their website, please understand that computer usage can be monitored and it is not always possible to clear your history or erase your "footprints", even if you think you have. If you have any doubts that you are being monitored, please call the hotline from a safe place. For more information you can visit the website at: www.thehotline.org.

Acknowledgments

How do you acknowledge a group of people who have stood by your side and, in essence, kept you alive, when you cannot even write a book using your real name? I suppose you do what you have always done, you put it out there in the hopes that the messages will find their way to the right people because that is what the universe intends to happen.

So, with that in mind, I would like to acknowledge the following people for helping me arrive to this day:

My mom – you have stood by my side on countless scary days and nights, helped to barricade my door, my heart, and my soul. You are a part of me that cannot be broken, and I a part of you. Together we are a force to be reckoned with. Dad would be very proud.

My dad – you're not here to see or read this. But I know you are still watching over me. You're mad as hell at what happened to your little girl and you cheer me on every time I get up and declare a new day. So I will keep doing that – for you and for everyone who needs me to.

My sister – it hurts you too much to know all of the truth so I only gave you what you could take. We are so close that we feel one another's pain. But you never left my side and you are still standing right here today making sure that I am ok. You are my best friend.

My brother and my sister-in-law and their children – there are no words to describe you that are short of incredible and powerful. You were the safety net that caught me every time he pushed me off the cliff. You didn't want to be there to see me fall but you had no choice but to catch me. Thank you for reminding me what family means, time and again.

My friends – I wish I could name each and every one of you! You helped me find a home when I had to run, you took my calls any time of the day or night, you cooked food for me and my children and made sure that we ate it, you checked in on us every single day, you watched me fall apart, put myself together, and fall apart again so many times that we all started looking for the missing pieces. You were the glue that finally held them together. I love you all.

he school staff and Principal - You know who you are. I can't put into words the difference you made in my life and the lives of my boys. You fed my soul when it was being starved to death, you protected me and kept me safe. You thought I was saving you, indeed it was quite the opposite.

My legal team, my courtroom witnesses, Judge B – You believed in me when he said I was crazy, when he said I was lying, and when he said things that even I believed even though they were not true. You helped me find my strength again at a time when I needed it the most, and reminded me that justice can still exist in this world. You were courageous and I will need you to be so again. Our legal system is not completely set up in support of victims yet. There is work to be done, let's go do that together.

My therapist –You have pulled me up from the trenches more times than I care to remember. And you never falter when we look forward and discover how much work is left to be done. You are a kind and gentle spirit that I am sure was meant to cross my path.

My "Media Guy" – I walked back into your life after decades and you didn't blink. You chuckled at the size of my aspirations and laughed as you said you knew I would "do it again." Your faith in me gives me confidence every day to keep on going.

My Editorial and Design Team – You are the comma to my run on sentence, the colors to my canvas. Thank you for helping to bring this dream to life in a magical way. Your belief in me gave me courage to keep moving forward. I can't wait to work with you again!

My Publicist – You started out as my colleague and ended up as a friend for life. Part editor, part strategist, and real life human being full of compassion and understanding, you brought this book to a level that it would not have reached simply by challenging me every step of the way. Now, let's go finish what we started and change the world.

And finally, to all the men out there – one in four women will become a victim of domestic abuse or violence in her lifetime. That means three out of four of you will honor and respect the women that you will fall in love with. You're the standard that we all need to live by as we build a better tomorrow. Thank you for that.

About the Author

SUSAN SPARKS is an author, a journalist, an advocate, and entrepreneur. She is also a SODA™: a Survivor of Domestic Abuse.

In college, courses in law and communication were Susan's focus, and she graduated with honors. Upon graduation, she combined her two passions and began her career as an investigative journalist, later working in The National Press Building where she reported, wrote and produced stories for national network news. Susan then transitioned to a career in IT, working in business development, operations, production, and product development.

Six years ago Susan gathered the courage to break free from her abusive situation, sustaining both injury and emotional scars that will last a lifetime. As part of the healing process, she has turned her time and attention directly to the cause of helping others who are in abusive situations. To accomplish this, she is working diligently to raise the volume of the conversation about domestic abuse.

Susan Sparks is the Principal of four enterprises, and one charity, all dedicated to helping people avoid, understand, and prevent domestic abuse; and she has built www.thesoda-pop.com as a home online where people can go for help, education, and to find a community of others who share the same story.

SPARKS IN LOVE, which she hopes will serve as both an educational and cautionary tale to everyone who reads it, is Susan's first book. Susan is currently working on three other books to further the cause and hopes to bring *SPARKS IN LOVE* to television soon.

Mom to two teenagers, Susan spends her spare time (what mom has spare time?) with friends and family, her new puppy, and dreaming about free time to travel!

CPSIA information can be obtained
at www.ICGtesting.com
Printed in the USA
FSHW01n1020201018